# Using the EFQM Excellence Model within healthcare:

# a practical guide to success

# Using the EFQM Excellence Model within healthcare:

# a practical guide to success

Sue Jackson
Excellence Development Facilitator
The Centre for Excellence Development: University of Salford, UK

Kingsham Press
Chichester

First Published 2001
by Kingsham   Press

Oldbury Complex
Marsh Lane
Easthampnett
Chichester PO18 OJW
West Sussex.
United Kingdom

Typeset in Agaramond


Printed and Bound by MPG Books
Bodmin
Cornwall
United Kingdom



**ISBN:   1- 902115- 8- 5**

British Library Cataloging in Publication Data
A catalogue record of this book is available from the British Library
Jackson,Sue.

# Acknowledgements

I have many people to thank for providing me with the opportunity to write this book.

Dr Henry Stahr, Director of The Centre for Excellence Development for giving me the opportunity to broaden my knowledge and experience in applying the EFQM Excellence Model within healthcare and for being such a constant source of support and inspiration.

Everyone I have met at Burton Hospitals for sharing their knowledge, fears and aspirations with me. In particular, David Anderson, Chief Executive and Chris Taylor, Clinical Governance Lead, who have both been role models for implementing the EFQM Excellence Model and have taken time to correct the relevant draft sections of text.

To everyone at Lockside Medical Centre for being so welcoming and enthusiastic about applying the EFQM Excellence Model into general practice. Thanks also to Dr Richard Bircher for taking time to correct the relevant draft sections of text.

Finally, thanks to my colleagues who excercised patience with me whilst I was writing the book and to everyone who has contributed to the knowledge, skills and experience I have gained.

# Table of contents

# Chapter 1
# Introduction

## Excellence in healthcare

Excellence in healthcare is a challenging concept and one that many healthcare professionals believe is not achievable for a variety of reasons. However the main constraint would seem to be that there is no one view of what excellence in healthcare is and so achieving it is impossible given that the basic ingredient, namely a workable definition is not available. To illustrate, when healthcare personnel (clinical and non-clinical) have been asked to define excellence their responses have included:

*'Meeting consumer expectations in the most ideal way, using available resources, according to set standards which are continually assessed and improved to take into account changing expectations.'*

*'Excellence is doing it right the first time and every time with equity and fairness and listening to constructive feedback and making appropriate changes to improve services and standards of delivery.'*

*'Maintaining an achievable level of excellence recognising that it is an ever increasing developing process.'*

What is interesting about these views is that they all propose that excellence has a fixed point irrespective of whether that point moves over time. Whereas in reality excellence is better viewed as a journey rather than a destination, particularly as the healthcare environment changes in response to new technologies, research, and the needs and expectations of patients, carers and other interested parties.

Another interesting feature to emerge from the above definitions is that healthcare personnel view excellence as only involving the customer or consumer. A view that suggests excellence is a goal to be pursued without considering the needs of the people delivering the service. Consequently the insight is one dimensional rather than holistic, a serious oversight when striving for healthcare excellence. Especially when no individual healthcare department and/or profession can deliver excellence alone and a happy workforce is conducive to delivering a quality service. By way of an explanation; a surgeon cannot perform an operation unless the theatre gowns and equipment are sterile; an outpatient appointment cannot go ahead (or should not go ahead) without the health records or a clean environment; healthcare employees will soon fail to provide a good quality service if they are not valued or paid appropriately and on time.

So from this limited analysis it can be seen that excellence is a dynamic, holistic concept that is difficult to pin down into one time frame or one dimension. Furthermore a one line definition is not available and some would argue does not need to be because valuable time is wasted on interpreting and/or agreeing a definition when it could be better spent delivering healthcare improvements (Smith 1986) and thereby taking appropriate action(s) towards excellence. This is an important feature in the pursuit of healthcare excellence as personal experience can confirm that time is currently being squandered debating the concept at the expense of making the healthcare environment better for customers, employees and other stakeholders. There can be no doubt that this debate demonstrates poor usage of vital healthcare resources.

However, Crosby (1980) does recognise that failing to define quality within an organisation is a problem and so the same can be applied for excellence. Particularly as omitting to agree a clear definition means that erroneous assumptions are adopted which adversely impacts on communications and progress. (Crosby 1980) The assumptions purported by Crosby (1980) include quality means luxury, quality is intangible and therefore not measurable, delivering quality costs money, and quality originates in the quality department. It would seem that these assumptions could be applied to excellence too. In other words: excellence means luxury, excellence is intangible and therefore not measurable, delivering excellence costs money, and excellence originates in the excellence department. If these assumptions are believed they can seriously compromise progress towards healthcare excellence and so need to be eradicated before the journey can commence.

## Excellence means luxury

Many healthcare personnel would agree that providing a luxury service is outside the bounds of current financial constraints. In public sector healthcare organisations providing luxury in some aspects of the service could only be achieved at the expense of providing a poor or no service in other areas of healthcare. Consequently providing luxury in a healthcare environment does not align to the values of the people working within it. It is no wonder that healthcare personnel with this view of excellence have no desire to support the delivery of it.

However, excellence is not about luxury. Fundamentally, it is about being customer focused and demonstrating continuous improvement in all the key aspects of the organisation. Other principles apply like 'right first time' and 'conformance to requirements' which basically mean that efforts are centred around minimising errors and meeting customer need. In healthcare these needs include a 'warm' smile, holding someone's hand, sending the right letter to the right person, providing the right treatment for the condition, performing the right test on a specimen and returning the result to the right department. When these basic ingredients are not in place, no healthcare customer, irrespective of any luxuries would feel their needs were being met. Hence, healthcare excellence relates completely to the values and expectations of healthcare personnel and the people they serve.

However, it should be noted that identifying customer needs accurately is reliant upon obtaining customer views of each healthcare organisation. Once this has been achieved each healthcare organisation can take steps to provide a service that reflects and 'conforms' to the needs and wishes of its customers, thereby reflecting the values of excellence.

## Excellence is intangible and therefore not measurable

Given that excellence involves doing things right first time and conforming to requirements the argument that this is not measurable is inaccurate. (Crosby 1980)

For instance, the number of times a specimen is sent to the wrong department, or the request form is completed incorrectly is tangible and measurable. Likewise, sending the right letter or appointment to the right person is tangible and measurable.

Furthermore, what constitutes a 'warm' smile and the value gained from holding someone's hand could be measured despite there being differences in the views of customers. It is just that measuring those perceptions is more challenging than measuring process outputs. Nevertheless, it does not imply that efforts should not be made to make these measurements, rather that they should be utilised to best effect. Particularly when it is widely recognised that 'what gets measured, gets attention', and meeting these basic needs of healthcare customers should be receiving attention and should be subject to continuous improvement in the pursuit of excellence.

## Delivering excellence costs money

The view that delivering excellence costs money is often linked with the view that excellence is luxury. When the definition that excellence is '*conformance to requirements*' (Crosby 1980) is applied it can be readily seen that achieving excellence saves money. One particular example that illustrates this point comes from a conversation with a community midwife who worked in a rural area. The midwife was explaining how busy she was and how she would love to visit the delivery suite each day before she went out on her visits. However, she never had [prioritised] the time to visit delivery suite and so was always unaware of women who had been admitted during the night.

Consequently some of the visits she performed were ineffectual because the women had been admitted to the delivery suite during the night and so were not at home. Hence the midwife chose to travel 25 miles to a house to find out whether the woman was at home or not, instead of visiting (or telephoning) the delivery suite each shift day morning. The costs incurred by performing an ineffectual visit far outweigh the alternative of 'doing things right first time', which is what Crosby (1980) was referring to when he maintained that '*quality is free*'.

## Excellence originates in the excellence department

The United Kingdom (UK) government maintained that '*Every part of the NHS, and everyone who works in it, should take responsibility for working to improve quality*'. (Department of Health 1998) The statement clearly recognises that in order to achieve excellence everyone in the organisation needs to be on board. Therefore achieving excellence in healthcare cannot be the sole responsibility of the excellence [quality] department.

Nevertheless, healthcare personnel cannot strive for excellence unless they have the skills to do that, a view that is shared by Wim Schellekens from the Dutch Institute for Healthcare Improvement. During his plenary presentation at the 5th European Forum for Quality Improvement in Healthcare (2000) he explained that '*bad quality is unnecessary suffering for patients*'. Wim Schellekens also asserted that providing a quality service meant healthcare professionals needed to be equipped with their specialist knowledge and expertise in addition to knowledge and expertise of total quality management and excellence.

Therefore the role of the excellence department is one of ensuring healthcare personnel have the necessary skills in the area of quality and excellence and then providing them with the support to apply those skills into practice. However, neither will be effective unless the organisation has some insight into what healthcare excellence means for them. Consequently healthcare personnel need to be familiar with the characteristics of healthcare excellence before they can continue the journey towards it.

## Characteristics of excellence in healthcare

Determining the characteristics of excellence in healthcare is easier than identifying an all-encompassing definition. This has been demonstrated during a number of workshops when healthcare personnel have readily identified features associated with excellent organisations. For instance, the feedback often contains the following words and statements:

**Customers**
- patients (customers) receive the treatment/service they need and want
- consumer expectations are identified and met
- customers perceive a good service
- equity
- fairness/listening
- looking at users views, tailor service to users' views and expectations,
- different expectations from provider consumer (providers view of quality can be different to the consumers)

**People**
- staff feel happy at work
- people (staff) feel involved in what is happening in the organisation

**Leadership**
- everyone in the whole organisation is working in the same direction
- there is a good management style
- communications are good

**Products and Services**
- the organisation can meet the ever changing demands of healthcare
- constant improvement
- dependability
- provide a high standard
- comparable

**Processes**
- performance is measured and improvements can be seen
- the work is carried out efficiently and effectively
- setting of standards
- right first time/every time

**Resources**
- good use of resources
- sufficient resources
- good information and data collection systems

**Principles**
- needs to be measurable

When the words or statements are examined and compared to the views of gurus in the field of quality and excellence it can be seen that all the above are features of an excellent healthcare organisation. However, a few more can be added. For instance, teamwork, empowerment, continuous cycle of improvement, meeting the needs of internal customers, recognising excellence is not an add-on and valuing staff views. (Peratec 1994) Crosby (1980) would also include, trust, a 'can do' attitude, a focus on system improvement and not on blaming people, the use of generic quality tools and good education and training.

All in all, the above characteristics which are in no-way exhaustive suggest that healthcare excellence is a multi-facetted endeavour that some would argue involves changing hearts and minds, thereby changing organisational culture. In particular John Denham was quoted as saying *'Patients must be able to make informed choices about their care and be confident that all aspects of their care will be equally good. ... This is about changing culture, attitudes and behaviours so that quality is integral to the way the NHS* [National Health Service] *works, not an optional extra'.* (McIntosh 1999)

Ardabell et al (1995) argues that changing a culture requires energy, commitment, clear vision, radical thinking, pain and chaos. So would healthcare benefit from concentrating its efforts and experiencing the pain required to achieve this culture change? Or are all the above characteristics already present in most healthcare organisations?

### Is there a need for healthcare excellence?

Within healthcare there are a number of examples that demonstrate a lack of characteristics associated with excellence. Although the author does recognise that there are also many incidences which demonstrate the total opposite. Nevertheless, there is an argument for pursing healthcare excellence, as a number of characteristics associated with excellence are not consistently present. The following examples confirm that inconsistency of products and services, inefficient processes, wasting resources, lack of knowledge and application regarding excellence principles, and inadequate performance management systems are features of healthcare practice.

### Example 1 - Lack of Customer focus

A couple of months prior to the event described below there had been an increase of thefts on a delivery suite and the solution implemented was to restrict visitors to the ward area. Labouring women were therefore instructed that they could only have one visitor whilst on the delivery suite. Not long after this *rule* had been applied an incident occurred whereby a labouring woman arrived at the delivery suite with her partner and her mother. The family was duly informed of the new rule *'only one visitor'*. However, the labouring woman had received previous promises that partner and mother could be present during her time on delivery suite.

Not happy with the broken promise the woman left the delivery suite choosing to have her baby at home with her partner and her mother beside her. With the care of the community midwife the delivery was safe albeit emotionally affected by the visiting rule incident. Consequently on this occasion there was a complete lack of customer focus and as a consequence the customer declined the service being offered.

## Example 2 - Products and services are inconsistent

An example from a clinician attending an excellence workshop highlighted an inconsistency amongst service provision. In essence what had happened was that a healthcare professional had taken some blood from a customer (patient) and labelled the specimen tube with a patient identification sticker. Consequently vital information was omitted which meant the laboratory could not undertake the relevant test. On this occasion a repeat blood sample had to be obtained which was unpleasant and inconvenient for the customer (patient), in addition to wasting healthcare resources regarding time and equipment. Furthermore, diagnosis and treatment were delayed, which resulted in a second adverse effect on the customer (patient).

## Example 3 – Inefficient processes

A further example from a healthcare professional attending a workshop highlighted that at one hospital a policy was in place whereby any child undergoing surgery had to be escorted into theatre and the anaesthetic room by a qualified nurse. However, at this hospital nurses were expressing repeated frustration because they were regularly being asked to take the children to the theatre area too early. It was not uncommon to wait between thirty and forty-five minutes in the theatre area prior to escorting the child into the anaesthetic room. This practice increased the anxiety amongst the children waiting for surgery and resulted in complaints from the children's parents who were waiting in the ward area. It also meant that a qualified nurse could be missing from the surgical ward for up to an hour at a time during which time colleagues had to respond to the complaints of parents in addition to dealing with a heavy workload minus a key member of the team.

## Example 4 – Wasting healthcare resources

A further example from a healthcare professional attending a workshop highlighted an incident that was similar to example 3 in that it was not uncommon. In this instance a district nurse was asked to visit a customer (patient) who had been discharged from a hospital ward. On arrival at the house the district nurse was informed that the address s/he had been given was incorrect. Consequently s/he had to drive to the nearest health centre to telephone the ward and ascertain the correct address. Dealing with this communication error took a minimum of thirty minutes.

## Example 5 – Limited knowledge of excellence concepts

During the early months of 2000, the author was delivering a workshop to senior managers and clinicians of a large NHS teaching hospital. The subject matter was the EFQM Excellence Model. During the workshop the delegates were informed of the fundamental principles of the Model including customer focus, leadership, management by processes and facts, people development and involvement, continuous learning, innovation and improvement, partnership development and public responsibility and how they related to healthcare. During this presentation one of the most senior members of the group interrupted the session to express that s/he had heard what had been said but that the language could be likened to that of '*an alien from the planet Zog*'. S/he also expressed concerns that healthcare was so far from this ideal that it was unrealistic to expect that excellence could be achieved in the current healthcare climate.

There were two main areas of concern that arose from this interjection. Firstly that the language of quality was so alien to this particular healthcare organisation that it implied customers' and employee needs were not being considered let alone met. And secondly that the leadership was so overwhelmed by the concept of excellence that it wasn't driving the values of total quality management.

## Example 6 - Inadequate performance measurement

The following quotes from the Health Service Journal indicate that UK healthcare would benefit from a more comprehensive performance measurement framework.

> '.. *volume-based throughput measures that assess such factors are only a small part of the picture*'. *Assessing performance, as we are coming to appreciate, is altogether a more complex activity. ...... Yet otherwise intelligent people, whether in the NHS, the media or higher education, persist in reducing such complexity to a handful of quantifiable measures which may in themselves be utterly meaningless or certainly fail to address the real issue of how best to establish effectiveness*'. (Hunter 1997)

> '*These findings add to a growing consensus that the present measurement of quality within healthcare is too narrow and is restrained by the ability of present systems to monitor solely quantitative data*'. (Wakeley 1997)

> '*Trust managers lack information on their consultants' activity levels, let alone the effectiveness and outcomes of their work*'. (Maynard and Sheldon 1997)

*'There is a risk that a performance indicator is chosen because it is easily measured and relates to current processes in which data is recorded rather than because it has validity'.* (Myers 1999)

## Transforming healthcare excellence from myth to reality

It would appear that there is a need for transforming healthcare excellence from its current myth into a reality. However, achieving this requires healthcare personnel to not only know and understand the tools of quality and excellence but also to apply them. (Wim Schellekens 5th European Forum for Quality Improvement in Healthcare)

Furthermore, it would appear that an overarching framework is needed that will support healthcare organisations to have in place all the characteristics associated with excellence, which include:

- a customer focus,
- valuing and involving employees,
- sound leadership,
- consistency in products and services,
- efficient processes,
- good use of resources,
- a rigorous, integrated performance measurement system that drives continuous improvement,
- teamwork,
- empowerment,
- high level of skills in quality and excellence,
- improvement, and
- a culture of trust and 'can do-ness'.

There is one such framework that is currently being more widely used within European healthcare and that is the European Foundation for Quality Management (EFQM) Excellence Model. This tool is well recognised in industry for being comprehensive, practical, easy to apply and rigorous enough to support the journey towards excellence. However, it has yet to be welcomed by most healthcare organisations, which is why this book is dedicated to enabling healthcare personnel to further their learning about the EFQM Excellence Model. The book is designed to provide practical guidance for healthcare personnel so that they can avoid the common pitfalls of using the EFQM Excellence Model within a healthcare environment thereby enhancing their likelihood of success.

Throughout this book it may be useful to remember that it is not the speed of the journey that matters but the direction.

# Chapter 2
# The EFQM Excellence Model

## Inception

The European Foundation for Quality Management (EFQM) Excellence Model was formally launched in 1991 in response to influential changes in business practices. These changes began soon after the second world war when the Japanese made huge efforts to regain their economy. One of the approaches was to start a quality movement, which the government did in 1946 via the creation of the Union of Japanese Scientists and Engineers (JUSE). By 1949 JUSE had formulated a Quality Control Research Group who provided lectures and education on the principles of quality control. Not long afterwards Dr W Edwards Deming, an American management consultant was invited to speak at a series of conferences and soon became involved in supporting Japanese companies to use self-assessment. By 1951 the Deming Prize was launched which meant Japanese businesses could apply for a national award based on their achievements towards using self-assessment as a tool for delivering better quality products and services.

As self-assessment became more widely used the Japanese economy went from strength to strength. So much so that by the end of the 1970's the quality of Japanese products exceeded that of Western manufacturers (Evans and Lindsay 1993) and the American economy was suffering from the impact. Recognising that American productivity was declining President Ronald Reagan commissioned a national study in October of 1982. The recommendations from this study were that America should initiate a national quality award similar to the Deming Prize. Consequently on 20th August 1987 the Malcolm Baldridge National Quality Award (MBNQA) was launched likewise based on a self-assessment framework.

The most interesting aspect of these events is that it took at least twenty years for the Japanese quality movement to impact on Western markets. This is a realistic indication of the length of time it takes to transform an organisation from one that pays lip service to quality into one that fully subscribes and practices by the principles of total quality management and excellence. Therefore the pursuit of excellence needs to be seen as a long term, permanent goal rather than a 'quick fix' solution to current issues.

Soon after the MBNQA was launched the presidents of 14 European companies joined together (1988) to form the European Foundation for Quality Management based in Brussels. The EFQM is a membership based not-for-profit organisation with the aim of making *'European Businesses more competitive through the application of TQM philosophy'.* (EFQM 1997) The EFQM, endorsed by the European Commission worked with the European Organisation for Quality to create the European Foundation for Quality Management Business Excellence Model. In October 1991, the European Quality Award (EQA) was launched using the EFQM Business Excellence Model self-assessment framework. The EQA was designed to increase awareness within European businesses that quality was growing in importance when competing in the global market place.

In the early 1990's the EFQM Business Excellence Model became widely used amongst European private sector service and production type organisations. However the situation was not repeated within the public sector which prompted the EFQM to create a Public and Voluntary sectors version of the Model. In 1996 a new European Award category was introduced for Public and Voluntary Sector organisations. Soon after this the EFQM commenced a major review to further improve the Model.

### Recent developments
Feedback from EFQM members showed that although the 1997 Model was extremely useful it could be improved upon to reflect the changes impacting on Europe-wide organisations. In particular the Model needed to take account of the increasing importance of managing partnerships and knowledge. A Europe-wide consultation exercise provided the EFQM with a wealth of suggestions for the nature and content of the changes required by users of the Model. Concept mapping was also employed to ensure that an improved Model truly reflected the needs of all organisations striving for excellence.

Members of EFQM maintained that the improved model needed to be:

- simple and easy to understand and use,
- holistic, covering all aspects of an organisation's activities and results,
- not unduly prescriptive,
- dynamic so as to accommodate changing demands,
- flexible and readily applicable for all types of organisations,
- clearly related to the previous Model so that transfer to the improved Model could be more smoothly effected. (EFQM website March 1999)

On 21st April 1999 the EFQM Excellence Model was launched, the most noticeable change being the removal of the word 'business'. The changed name was to reflect the Model's applicability to all sectors and organisations whether private, public or not for profit. The improved Model also made the links between enablers and results more explicit in addition to replacing the blue card scoring system with the RADAR logic. Nevertheless, the fundamental principles, overall approach and structure of the Model remained the same.

## Fundamental principles of the EFQM Excellence Model
Underpinning the EFQM Excellence Model are 8 fundamental principles (EFQM 1999), the order of which do not reflect any particular significance:

### Results orientation
Achieving excellence has many dimensions and so cannot just be about balancing a budget and increasing productivity or throughput. Therefore organisations need to balance and satisfy the needs of all their relevant stakeholders (e.g. customers, people employed by the organisation, society in general, governments, statutory organisations) and clearly show that they are doing this.

### Customer focus
The customer is the final arbitrator of the products and services provided and therefore excellent organisations need to focus on meeting the current and future needs of their existing and potential customers. In some, if not most instances, customers also want reassurances that their chosen provider is achieving good results, which further strengthens the need for a results orientation.

### Leadership and constancy of purpose
In order to achieve excellence, leaders in all areas of the organisation need to behave in such a way that they create a clarity and unity of purpose in addition to ensuring an environment in which the organisation and its people can excel.

### Management by processes and facts
Understanding the different aspects of all the organisation's processes and always endeavouring to improve them is necessary for achieving excellence. To do this requires reliable information from wider sources than the process, in particular the perceptions (views) of all relevant stakeholders (customers, people employed by the organisation, society in general and/or governments).

### People development and involvement
Realising the full potential of the organisation's people is necessary for achieving excellence and releasing this potential is best achieved through

shared values and a culture of trust, empowerment and teamwork. No one person can achieve organisational excellence.

### Continuous learning, innovation and improvement

Excellence is an ever-moving destination, which requires a continuous cycle of learning, innovation and improvement. Organisational performance is enhanced when knowledge is managed and widely shared in a culture supportive of continuous improvement.

### Partnership and development

An organisation is more likely to achieve excellence if it develops trusting, mutually beneficial relationships with its partners. These partners can be internal or external to the organisation providing the emphasis is on mutual benefit, sharing of knowledge and integration.

### Public responsibility

A feature of an excellent organisation would be that it manages its long-term impact on society in an ethical manner. Exceeding expectations and statutory regulations of the community at large are implicit within excellent organisational practices.

### Approach

'The EFQM Excellence Model is a non-prescriptive framework that recognises there are many approaches to achieving sustainable excellence'. (EFQM Web-site June 1999) '*Non-prescriptive*' in this sense means that there is no one way of achieving excellence. Rather many approaches will attain similar outcomes because they are applied in different cultural, economic and social contexts.

The EFQM believe that central to achieving organisational excellence is a process known as self-assessment, defined by the EFQM as; '*A comprehensive, systematic and regular review of an organisation's activities and results referenced against the EFQM Excellence Model*'. (EFQM 1999b) In essence this definition recognises that achieving excellence requires an organisation to have a cyclic, not an ad-hoc process for determining the impact of its approaches on overall performance. The self-assessment process also needs to encompass *all* the key elements of the organisation rather than only a minority of them. Review implies that further assessments will need to be undertaken in order to monitor the effect of the continuous improvement actions. Self-assessing against a model of excellence indicates that an organisation will have an internal view of its overall performance in addition to an external perspective based on the performance of other similar and/or best in class organisations. Using a model like the EFQM Excellence Model enables an organisation to benchmark like with like which can act as a motivator towards excellence status.

Self-assessment also means that the people within the organisation or department (not an outside assessor or auditor) identify their own performance in relation to the model framework. Once they have gathered and analysed the data regarding their performance they are able to determine whether they are performing well in this particular area (strength) or whether they are not performing as well as they would like (area for improvement) providing specific targets have been set.

Obviously self-assessment involves the collection of meaningful, timely and accurate data which gives a true picture of the organisation's performance thereby dispelling 'gut feelings' and any other inaccuracies associated with the individual views of the organisation's stakeholders. The ideal situation to be in is one whereby adverse trends can be identified and acted upon well in advance of any symptoms, for instance rising sickness absence figures that could impact on the morale of the employees and the customers' experience of the service.

### Structure

The EFQM Excellence Model is diagrammatically represented as nine boxes. (See Figure 2.1) Each box depicts one of the self-assessment criteria of the Model.

**Figure 2.1 The EFQM Excellence Model (EFQM1999a)**

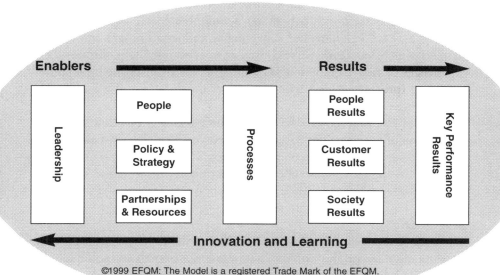

©1999 EFQM: The Model is a registered Trade Mark of the EFQM.

## Criteria

Of the nine criteria, 5 are enablers (describing how things are done in the organisation) and 4 are results (describing what is achieved by the enablers). The five enabler criteria are: Leadership, Policy and Strategy, People, Partnerships and Resources and Processes, and the four results criteria are Customers, People, Society and Key Performance. The overall philosophy is that *'Excellent results with respect to Performance, Customers, People and Society are achieved through Leadership driving Policy and Strategy, People, Partnerships and Resources, and Processes'*. (EFQM Web-site June 1999)

Readers who are familiar with the Donabedian (1980) approach to quality assessment may recognise the similarities between the EFQM Excellence Model and Donabedian's *'Structure, Process and Outcome'*. For instance Donabedian (1980) related 'Structure' to the tools and resources (human, physical and financial) of an organisation which can be aligned to the 'Leadership, Policy and Strategy, People and Partnership and Resources' criteria of the EFQM Excellence Model. 'Process' readily aligns to the processes criterion and 'Outcome' to the four results criteria (Customers, People, Society and Key Performance Results) of the EFQM Excellence Model.

The fundamental differences between the two approaches are that Donabedian's (1980) is based on standard setting and the EFQM Excellence Model on continuous improvement. The former therefore has a fixed destination which when reached can remove the stimulus for improving quality, whereas the latter has no fixed end point and so the stimulus to get better and/or become the best is potentially ingrained into everyday practice.

In addition the EFQM Excellence Model encourages 'organisations' to understand the relationship between actions (enablers) and results. An example may be designing and delivering an induction programme (people enabler) which has demonstrated a positive effect on the perceptions and experiences of new members of staff (people result), or changing a clinical procedure (process enabler) which improves the cure rate of a disease (key performance result).

Each of the nine criteria has a definition which provides a high level explanation of the particular criterion. To develop the high level meaning each criterion is supported by a number of sub-criteria (EFQM 1999a) to which an organisation applies self-assessment and continuous improvement actions in order to work towards excellence.

## Sub-criteria

There are 32 sub-criteria within the EFQM Excellence Model, 24 within the enablers and 8 within the results. These sub-criteria pose a series of questions that should be considered during the self-assessment process. Below each sub-criterion is a list or a number of lists that contain possible areas to address. These areas to address are not exhaustive or mandatory rather their intention is to provide further explanation and meaning for the particular sub-criterion. Given below is the actual definition of each of the nine criteria along with the relevant sub-criteria questions contained within the Public and Voluntary Sectors version of the EFQM Excellence Model. (EFQM 1999a) An indication of some possible healthcare areas to address developed by the author is also given.

## Leadership (Criterion 1)

The EFQM definition is *'How leaders develop and facilitate the achievement of the mission and vision, develop values required for long term success and implement these via appropriate actions and behaviours, and are personally involved in ensuring that the organisation's management system is developed and implemented'.*

*Sub-criteria*
Leadership covers four sub-criteria (1a – 1d) that **should** be addressed.

*1a  Leaders develop the mission, vision and values and are role models of a culture of Excellence*
Possible healthcare areas to address could include:
- developing the vision for the organisation;
- assessing, reviewing and improving leadership effectiveness in relation to excellence.

*1b  Leaders are personally involved in ensuring the organisation's management system is developed, implemented and continuously improved*
Possible healthcare areas to address could include:
- developing an organisational management structure that supports the policy and strategy;
- ensuring a robust system is in place for managing and improving the management of key processes.

*1c  Leaders are involved with customers, partners and representatives of society*
Possible healthcare areas to address could include:
- visiting clinical areas and establishing the views of patients;
- contributing to professional conferences and other partnership activities.

*1d  Leaders motivate, support and recognise the organisation's people*
Possible healthcare areas to address could include:

- being available to listen, support and recognise in a timely manner employees and other contributors of healthcare i.e. voluntary workers;
- enabling people to achieve their aspirations and organisational targets.

## Policy and Strategy (Criterion 2)

The EFQM definition is *'How the organisation implements its mission and vision via a clear stakeholder focused strategy, supported by relevant policies, plans, objectives, targets and processes'.*

*Sub-criteria*
Policy and Strategy covers five sub-criteria (2a – 2e) that **should** be addressed.

*2a Policy and Strategy are based on the present and future needs and expectations of stakeholders*
Possible healthcare areas to address could include:
- utilising government directives, for example the NHS Plan, Working Lives, National Service Frameworks and National Institute of Clinical Excellence recommendations, to determine policy and strategy:
- information relating to the needs of patients and other customers of healthcare.

*2b Policy and Strategy are based on information from performance measurement, research, learning and creativity related activities*
Possible healthcare areas to address could include:
- using information from internal processes like care pathways;
- applying research based practice and technological advances within healthcare.

*2c Policy and Strategy are developed, reviewed and updated*
Possible healthcare areas to address could include:
- incorporating risk management strategies:
- aligning policy and strategy to the fundamental principles of the EFQM Excellence Model.

*2d Policy and Strategy are deployed through a framework of key processes*
Possible healthcare areas to address could include:
- identify key process owners;
- reviewing and improving the organisation's approach to managing key processes.

*2e Policy and Strategy are communicated and implemented*

Possible healthcare areas to address could include:
- using team brief for communicating policy and strategy;
- agreeing action plans and timescales for delivering policy and strategy.

## People (Criterion 3)

The EFQM definition is *'How the organisation manages, develops and releases the knowledge and full potential of its people at an individual, team-based and organisation-wide level, and plans these activities in order to support its policy and strategy and the effective operation of its processes'.*

### Sub-criteria

People covers five sub-criteria (3a-3e) that **should** be addressed.

### 3a People resources are planned, managed and improved

Possible healthcare areas to address could include:
- agreeing the process for recruiting staff;
- ensuring fair employment practices.

### 3b People's knowledge and competencies are identified, developed and sustained

Possible healthcare areas to address could include:
- agreeing training plans and maximising training opportunities;
- activities associated with Investors in People accreditation.

### 3c People are involved and empowered

Possible healthcare areas to address could include:
- involving people in decision making;
- enabling people to utilise their initiative.

### 3d People and the organisation have a dialogue

Possible healthcare areas to address could include:
- identifying preferred methods of communication;
- utilising preferred methods of communication.

### 3e People are rewarded, recognised and cared for

Possible healthcare areas to address could include:
- quality award schemes and thank you letters;
- identifying and implementing flexible ways of working.

## Partnerships and Resources (Criterion 4)

The EFQM definition is *'How the organisation plans and manages its external partnerships and internal resources in order to support its policy and strategy and the effective operation of its processes'.*

## Sub-criteria
Partnerships and Resources covers five sub-criteria (4a-4e) that **should** be addressed.

### 4a External partnerships are managed
Possible healthcare areas to address could include:
- working with the local Health Authority, NHS Trusts, Local Authority and other public services;
- agreeing joint action plans.

### 4b Finances are managed
Possible healthcare areas to address could include:
- monthly monitoring of finances;
- managing financial risks.

### 4c Buildings, equipment and materials are managed
Possible healthcare areas to address could include:
- asset management;
- recycling and incinerating waste.

### 4d Technology is managed
Possible healthcare areas to address could include:
- adopting new medical technologies;
- using and replacing outdated technologies to improve healthcare.

### 4e Information and knowledge are managed
Possible healthcare areas to address could include:
- ensuring everyone has access to relevant information and knowledge;
- valuing creativity and innovation.

## Processes (Criterion 5)
The EFQM definition is *'How the organisation designs, manages and improves its processes in order to support its policy and strategy and fully satisfy, and generate increasing value for, its customers and other stakeholders'.*

## Sub-criteria
Processes covers five sub-criteria (5a-5e) that **should** be addressed.

*5a    Processes are systematically designed and managed*
Possible healthcare areas to address could include:
*   utilising the concept of integrated care pathways;
*   working with general practitioners, Trusts or health authorities to streamline processes.

*5b    Processes are improved, as needed, using innovation in order to fully satisfy and generate increasing value for customers and other stakeholders*
Possible healthcare areas to address could include:
*   piloting new processes;
*   ensuring people have the skills to apply the new or improved process.

*5c    Products and Services are designed and developed based on customer needs and expectations*
Possible healthcare areas to address could include:
*   using patient survey information to improve healthcare delivery;
*   agreeing new ways of working in relation to expressed customer expectations.

*5d    Products and Services are produced, delivered and serviced*
Possible healthcare areas to address could include:
*   agreeing theatre lists and referral patterns;
*   considering the implementation elements associated with new clinical treatments.

*5e    Customer relationships are managed and enhanced*
Possible healthcare areas to address could include:
*   complaints handling;
*   changing outpatient appointments in line with patients' needs.

## Customer Results (Criterion 6)
The EFQM definition is *'What the organisation is achieving in relation to its external customers'.*

*Sub-criteria*
Customer Results covers two sub-criteria (6a-6b) that **should** be addressed.

*6a    Perception Measures*
These measures are of the customers' perceptions of the organisation (obtained, for example, from customer surveys, focus groups, vendor ratings, compliments and complaints). In relation to healthcare, customer perception

measures **may** include those relating to:
- accessing healthcare;
- satisfaction with treatment options and information;
- attitude of staff;
- catering, sign-posting and car parking.

### 6b  Performance Indicators

These measures are the internal ones used by the organisation in order to monitor, understand, predict and improve the performance of the organisation and to predict perceptions of its external customers. In relation to healthcare, performance indicators for customers **may** include those relating to:
- number of patient complaints;
- waiting times;
- percentage of contracts lost.

## People Results (Criterion 7)

The EFQM definition is *'What the organisation is achieving in relation to its people'.*

### Sub-criteria

People Results covers two sub-criteria (7a-7b) that **should** be addressed.

### 7a  Perception Measures

These measures are of the people's perception of the organisation (obtained, for example, from surveys, focus groups, interviews, structured appraisals). People perception measures in healthcare **may** include those relating to:
- job security;
- duty rotas;
- communication within the organisation;
- leadership style(s).

### 7b  Performance Indicators

These measures are the internal ones used by the organisation in order to monitor, understand, predict and improve the performance of the organisation's people and to predict their perceptions. In relation to healthcare, performance indicators for people **may** include those relating to:
- sickness absence rates;
- average number of training days per employee;
- vacancy rates;
- number of annual leave requests turned down.

## Society Results (Criterion 8)

The EFQM definition is *'What the organisation is achieving in relation to local, national and international society as appropriate'.*

*Sub-criteria*

Society Results covers two sub-criteria (8a-8b) that **should** be addressed.

*8a Perception Measures*

These measures are of the society's perception of the organisation (obtained, for example, from surveys, reports, public meetings, public representatives, governmental authorities). In relation to healthcare, society perception measures **may** include those relating to:

- response from sharing views regarding capital development programmes;
- noise levels;
- local car parking.

*8b Performance Indicators*

These measures are the internal ones used by the organisation in order to monitor, understand, predict and improve the performance of the organisation and to predict perceptions of society. In relation to healthcare, performance indicators for society **may** include those listed under **8a** and in addition:

- ratio of positive to negative media coverage;
- number of awards or accolades;
- number of new treatments launched.

## Key Performance Results (Criterion 9)

The EFQM definition is *'What the organisation is achieving in relation to its planned performance'.*

*Sub-criteria*

Key Performance Results covers the following two sub-criteria that **should** be addressed. Depending on the purpose and objectives of the organisation some of the measures contained in the guidance for Key Performance Outcomes may be applicable to Key Performance Indicators and vice versa.

*9a Key Performance Outcomes*

These measures are key results planned by the organisation which, in relation to healthcare, **may** include those relating to:

- balancing the budget;
- mortality rates;
- survival rates for cancer;
- compliance with maintenance legislation.

### 9b Key Performance Indicators

These measures are the operational ones used in order to monitor, understand, predict and improve the organisation's likely key performance outcomes. In relation to healthcare, they **may** include those relating to:

- income generated;
- percentage of patients receiving thrombolysis within 30minutes of admission;
- inappropriate referral rate;
- turnaround time for maintenance jobs.

Within the Public and Voluntary Sectors version of the EFQM Excellence Model booklet is a glossary of terms that further helps understanding of the Model criteria, sub-criteria and areas to address. Additionally, the booklet contains information relating to the evaluation tools that can be used with the Model, namely the pathfinder card and the RADAR logic. (EFQM 1999a)

## RADAR logic

At the heart of the EFQM Excellence Model lies a 'logic' known as **RADAR**. (EFQM 1999a) The RADAR logic consists of the following elements: **R**esults, **A**pproach, **D**eployment, **A**ssessment and **R**eview. (See Figure 2.2) In order to fulfil the requirements of the RADAR logic an organisation needs to:

- Determine the financial, operational and stakeholder (customer, people, society, governments, statutory bodies etc) perception results it is aiming for,
- Plan and develop a 'sound' Approach or approaches for achieving the proposed results,
- Deploy the approaches in a systematic way so that full integration of them is achieved, and
- Assess and Review the approaches by undertaking regular measurement, which in turn promotes learning and leads to improvement activities where necessary.

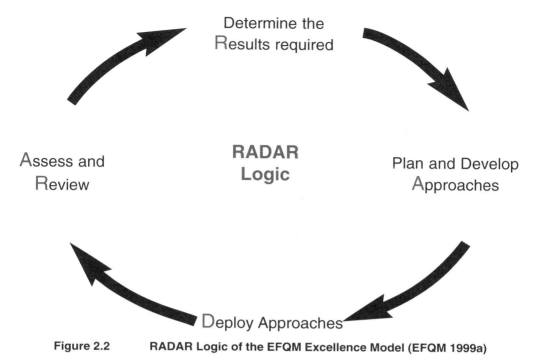

**Figure 2.2**     **RADAR Logic of the EFQM Excellence Model (EFQM 1999a)**

In essence, the EFQM Excellence model subscribes to the continuous improvement cycle of Dr W Edwards Deming (1982), namely the 'Plan, Do, Check and Act' cycle. And, given that the process is driven by self- assessment Porter and Tanner (1996) maintain that it is an excellent opportunity to integrate total quality management into normal, everyday operations, a philosophy that EFQM aim to fully promote.

With regards to the specific elements of the RADAR logic the EFQM Excellence Model defines excellence in results as those which:

- show positive trends and/or sustained good performance,
- are meeting appropriate targets,
- compare well with other organisations,
- are caused by the enablers (actions), and
- can demonstrate that the scope of the results address the relevant areas of the organisation. (EFQM 1999a)

There is an appreciation that 'one-off' good results, in a limited number of areas, is more readily achieved than sustained positive performance in a wider span of areas, but the latter is more indicative of an excellent organisation. Following on from the previous example relating to the induction of new members of staff the results would need to demonstrate a consistent, positive trend in the perceptions of new employees (people results) to the organisation. Furthermore, when considering one aspect of the scope element of the Model, the organisation would probably measure error rates for payroll (key performance results), and demonstrate an ongoing reduction in these, as corporate induction may be designed to undertake all the necessary administrative duties on the first day of employment.

Excellence in the approaches is determined when there is evidence of:
- a clear rationale for the planned approach,
- well defined and developed processes which are clearly focused on stakeholder (customers, people, society, governments and/or statutory organisations) needs,
- integration with the organisation's policy and strategy, and
- linkage with other approaches where appropriate.

Again relating this to the induction of new members of staff example, the rationale would be to welcome new employees into the organisation. The regularity and content of the induction programme would reflect the needs of these new employees and be integrated into the organisation's policy and strategy towards being a good employer. Furthermore there would be an obvious linkage with other recruitment and retention approaches designed to meet the needs of the organisation's people.

In terms of deployment, excellence status is attained when the approach has been systemically implemented in all the relevant areas. For the induction of new members of staff example, a system would need to be in place for ensuring that all new members of staff are invited and able to attend the induction programme.

Achieving excellence status is even more rigorous when the assessment and review element of the RADAR logic is applied. In particular, excellent organisations must demonstrate that they have applied assessment and review to both the approach and the deployment of that approach. The EFQM also maintains that the assessment and review processes must ensure that there is a regular measurement system in place from which learning can occur. Once the measures and subsequent learning is available the output from both must be used to identify, plan and implement improvement actions. (EFQM 1999a)

Going back to the induction of new members of staff example this would mean that the organisation collects data that would indicate whether the programme was achieving the desired results of improving people's perceptions of being welcomed and of reducing the number of payroll errors. Measures would also be taken to determine whether *all* new members of staff had been invited and able to attend the induction programme. In terms of learning, once the measures were available, the relevant process owners would be able to see whether the enabler was effective. If it was, no changes to the enabler would be necessary (and there is a rationale for that). However, if it was not, the process owner would be able to determine whether it was due to the approach itself or to the deployment of that approach.

For instance, there could be a perfectly good approach in place that is poorly deployed, or alternatively a poor approach in place that is fully deployed. Either way the learning that emerges from identifying the impact of this enabler can be applied to designing and implementing improvement actions. Once the corrective actions have been put into effect the cycle of measurement, learning and improvement would begin again, thereby creating a culture of continuous improvement towards organisational excellence.

Once organisations have attained this level of rigour into their normal day to day practices they may consider applying for the European Quality Award or a National Quality Award based on the EFQM Excellence Model. An example would be the UK (United Kingdom) Quality Award. To do this the organisation would need to be familiar with and using the scoring element of the EFQM Excellence Model.

**RADAR scoring matrix**

The RADAR scoring matrix is the evaluation method used for scoring applications for the European and other National Quality Awards based on the EFQM Excellence Model (EFQM 1999a). Organisations may also choose to apply the RADAR scoring matrix to objectively monitor their progress towards excellence and to support benchmarking with other organisations.

**Criteria weightings**

When an organisation is scored using the EFQM Excellence Model RADAR scoring matrix weights, in the form of percentages, are given to the nine criteria of the Model. (See Figure 2.3)

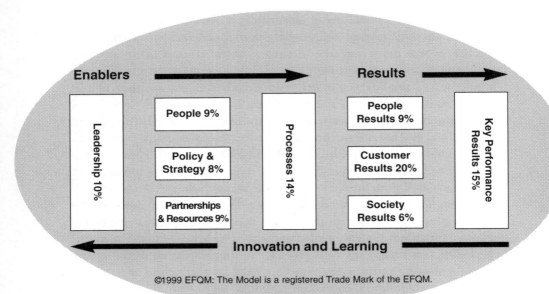

**Figure 2.3  The EFQM Excellence Model showing the weightings for each criterion (EFQM 1999a)**

The percentages shown in the enablers and results boxes are those that emerged from the values and experiences of the 14 founder member businesses of the EFQM.

What is interesting is that these weightings remained the same despite the extensive consultation exercise undertaken with all members of the EFQM during 1997 to 1999 (over 800 at that time).

When the Model weightings are examined it can be seen that the enablers and the results carry equal weights of 50%. Therefore according to the EFQM the 'How things are done' in an organisation are equally as important as 'What is achieved'. Secondly, it can be seen that the customer results carries the highest individual weighting (20%) of any of the nine criteria. This implies that meeting customer needs is paramount for achieving organisational excellence, a philosophy that reflects' the views of a number of gurus including Juran (1988) who maintained that quality is:

*'Fitness for purpose (as perceived by customers)'.*

The organisation's people also rate highly in achieving excellence as the People enabler and People Results criteria jointly amount to 18% of the Model scoring matrix. Further evidence that the EFQM Excellence Model is founded upon total quality management (TQM) principles. Particularly as the gurus advocate involvement, empowerment and teamwork are essential ingredients for securing a total quality management culture. (Deming 1982, Juran 1988)

Processes are weighted (14%) fairly high in the Model too, which recognises that an indicator of an excellent organisation is its attention to detail in relation to designing its processes around the needs of the customer. Right first time concepts fit in well here along with minimal duplication and delays.

Society results, which involve recycling materials, minimising energy usage and being involved in the local community carry the lowest weighting (6%), which many organisations feel comfortable with. However, it may not be appropriate for all organisations, as this aspect may be more important for some industries like those working in the field of Nuclear Fuel. Nevertheless, these weightings are applied to all organisations irrespective of the nature of their business and have been well accepted by them as can be seen from the number and the diversity of businesses applying for the quality awards based on the EFQM Excellence Model.

A question that is often asked is whether the percentages relate to the amount of effort that is required in each area in order to achieve excellence. However, the answer is 'No' because the effort required for each criteria is relative to the strengths and areas for improvement identified by the self-assessment. Therefore if the organisation is good at meeting customer needs and expectations, but does this at the expense of the morale and satisfaction of its people, then clearly improvement efforts need to be concentrated more on people than on customers. However, the organisation will not be able to remove all efforts relating to customer satisfaction as it could be in danger of reversing the results, happy people but unhappy customers. This provides a further example that the Model is not prescriptive. It cannot be, because the achievements and characteristics of organisations differ and so reaching a common level of attainment will take varying degrees of effort in varying areas of management.

## Scoring sub-criteria

The first step towards scoring is to apply the RADAR scoring matrix to individual sub-criterion. To do this the assessor needs to consider the relevant elements of the RADAR scoring matrix. For instance scoring the results relates to the 'R' element of the RADAR logic which are scored against five elements; trends, targets, comparisons, causes and scope (see the section that defines excellent results on page 25). Percentage scores are assigned to these elements based on the evidence available. In summary the range is from 'No results or anecdotal information' to 'Excellent results' the former of which would score 0% and the latter a possible 100%. For more information on scoring results refer to the Public and Voluntary Sectors version of the EFQM Excellence Model handbook. (EFQM 1999a)

Scoring the enablers relates to the 'ADAR' elements of the RADAR logic. An approach is scored against two aspects (sound and integrated), deployment also against two aspects (implemented and systematic) and assessment and review against three aspects (measurement, learning and improvement). The range is from 'No evidence or anecdotal' to 'Comprehensive evidence', the former of which would score 0% and the latter a possible 100%. For more information on scoring enablers refer to the Public and Voluntary Sectors version of the EFQM Excellence Model handbook. (EFQM 1999a)

The maximum score that can be attained is 1,000 points, although no organisation to date has come anywhere near this level. Organisations winning the European Quality Award tend to score around 600 – 700 points, which demonstrates the rigor of the Model. Furthermore organisations attaining a high score one year may not be able to replicate the score a year later because the organisations with whom they compared favourably to previously may have risen the excellence stakes, a scenario which clearly indicates how dynamic the EFQM Excellence Model is.

When the RADAR scoring matrix is applied for the first time, it can appear very subjective to a new assessor and/or team using the EFQM Excellence Model. However, once the assessor/team is aware of what to look for and applies that learning into practice the comprehensive, rigorous nature of the Model soon becomes apparent. No more so than when a trained assessor is scoring an organisation that has applied for a Quality Award based on the EFQM Excellence Model.

**Quality awards based on the EFQM Excellence Model**
Since 1991 the EFQM have extended their quality award application criteria from solely businesses to the Public Sector in 1996 and to Operational Units (significant parts of companies that are not eligible to enter as a business) in 1997. To win the EQA, organisations need to be exceptional and the '*most successful exponents of the principles of Excellence in Europe within their category*'. Previous award winners include; Rank Xerox (1992), Milliken European Division (1993), D2D (Design to Distribution) Ltd (1994), Texas Instruments (1995), Brisa (1996), SGS-Thomson Microelectronics (1997), TNT United Kingdom (1998), Yellow Pages (1999), Nokia Mobile Phones, Europe and Africa (2000). Despite launching the Public Sector award category in 1996 (first winner could have been in 1997), there has only been one award winner in this category which was Inland Revenue, Accounts Office, Cumbernauld, Scotland in the year 2000. (EFQM 2000)

Organisations not attaining this level of excellence can be awarded prize winner status if they are able to demonstrate that their approach to quality management has significantly contributed to satisfying the expectations of their customers, employees and other stakeholders. Previous prize winners include BOC Limited, Special Gases (1992), Ericsson SA (1994), British Telecom (1996), Inland Revenue, Cumbernauld (1998) and Foxdenton School and Integrated Nursery (2000). Commencing 2001, EFQM are introducing a new award category that will recognise 'Achievement in Excellence', which will be awarded to organisations that can demonstrate they are well managed and aspiring to achieve role model status. (EFQM 2000)

The timing of the awards differ slightly in each country although the key steps in the process remain the same, (See Figure 2.4). An interesting feature of the process is that once an award assessor has undergone the training, this does not entitle them to be an award assessor for future years. Hence each award assessor has to complete the training each year if they are to contribute to the process. The reason for this is that a team of six people assesses each application and part of the training programme is dedicated to team development so that each assessor will feel comfortable to share her/his interpretation of the application with the remainder of the team. Consequently no same team of individuals comes together again because assessors are selected from a number of applications from individuals whose company and/or personal development has identified a need to experience the role of award assessor.

A further important factor is that each assessor has to sign a declaration that they have no interest in the company they are assessing and that they will not breach any confidentiality clauses. This has to be effected before the individual assessor is aware of the company they are going to assess. Finally, being an award assessor can involve up to 120 hours of work if the organisation is worthy of a site visit, and cost the individual or the organisation approximately £1,000 to fund the expenses associated with the training, consensus scoring exercise and site visit planning.

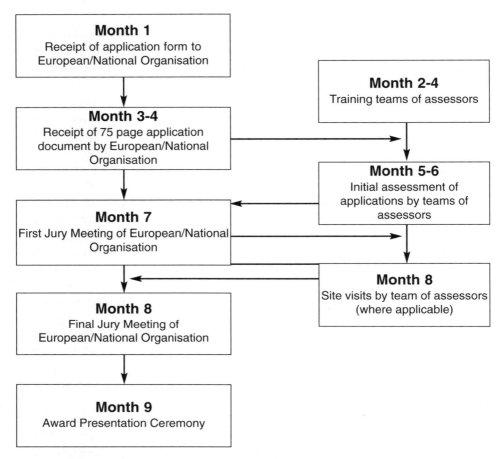

**Figure 2.4 Example of steps in a European/National Quality Award Process**

### Benefits to the organisation of becoming an award assessor

According to the EFQM (2000) the benefits of applying for the European Quality Award include:

- sharpening the focus of the organisation and its improvement activities,
- fostering teamwork as working towards a tight schedule provides people with clear aims and objectives,
- a heightened awareness of organisational excellence and the part quality management plays in its achievement,
- creating a succinct description of the organisation in terms of its enablers and results which is valuable in the contexts of communication, promotion and training,
- the feedback report that has been prepared by a team of independent assessors, senior managers and experts across Europe.

The feedback report contains an objective summary of key messages relating to the Model criteria and a list of strengths and areas for improvement for each of the 32 sub-criteria. This external, expert view can be very useful for identifying and prioritising future improvement actions.

However, judging from personal experience as an assessor, not all organisations experience the same level of benefits purported by the EFQM. For instance the feedback reports are not always as useful to the organisation as they might be. Content varies dependent upon the expertise and insight of the team of assessors. Some contain very enlightening, useful information and some contain nothing new or thought provoking for the applicant.

Another questionable feature is that of fostering teamwork as this can depend upon who is driving the organisation's application and the reasons behind it. So, should an influential individual (Chief Executive or Director) be pushing for the organisation to apply for an excellence award and the motives are seen as being more beneficial to the individual than the organisation, teamwork will not be fostered. Rather there will be resentment amongst the organisation's people and a feeling that senior managers are not walking the talk.

Despite these drawbacks, there is evidence that organisations do realise the benefits espoused by the EFQM. In particular one organisation, whilst preparing the submission document, recognised some gaps in performance that had not been evident previously. As a consequence corrective actions were extended to transform the areas for improvement into strengths as they were seen to be of significant benefit to overall company performance. By way of an illustration, one of the gaps identified was that its purchasing function was not systematic and so a purchasing manager was appointed to correct this.

Significant benefits were also realised from the site visit as the organisation felt a renewed sense of enthusiasm and commitment for its quality journey resulting in increased energy towards improvement efforts. Everyone became involved in the site visit and the profile of quality and organisational excellence was raised for quite some time after the application process had ended.

Another benefit, which supports the view of the EFQM is that once the 75-page application document is prepared there becomes available a very comprehensive overview of the organisation's approaches and achievements which can be utilised in a variety of ways. For instance it can be summarised and given to new members of staff, prospective customers and existing staff in support of good communications. However, the organisation is not the only beneficiary of the award application process as the individual assessor also undergoes a value-adding experience.

**Benefits to the individual of becoming an award assessor**

A noticeable omission from the Award Application document (EFQM 2000) is that it does not contain any reference to the individual assessor benefiting from the process. However, personal experience suggests that there are many benefits to be gained from the process. For instance, the award assessor training equips the individual with one of the prerequisites to provide licensed assessor training.

In addition understanding of the Model concepts and its application is deepened by each step of the award process. To illustrate, reading the applicant's submission document exposes the assessor to real-life examples of applying the concepts in another organisation. Secondly, undergoing team consensus gives the assessor the opportunity to debate the Model concepts and personal interpretations of them with other members of the assessment team. An unexpected spin off from undertaking the role of award assessor was an ability to write a better award submission document.

Networking is enhanced as usually the assessment teams are made up of individuals from diverse employment backgrounds. Personal experience involved working in a team that was made up of a senior manager from:

- British Nuclear Fuels with expertise in Policy and Strategy,
- Rover Group with expertise in process management,
- the Benefits Agency with expertise in Human Resources,
- the Police Force with expertise in implementing the EFQM Excellence Model,
- healthcare and academia with expertise in knowledge management, and
- British Aerospace with expertise in Leadership.

Consequently the opportunities for benchmarking, learning and personal development were immense.

If the assessment team are fortunate enough to score an application that is a potential award or prize winner then the benefits are increased. To explain, in this situation the assessment team have to undertake a site visit, which means each assessor is exposed to a series of best practices. Personal experience found that this was the best work experience ever encountered. Furthermore, the examples of best practice were very impressive and thought provoking and stimulated personal efforts towards own employing organisation's pursuit of excellence.

To provide some sort of flavour of these examples a summary of best practices are provided below under the relevant Model criteria heading.

## Leadership

The leaders within the organisation made great efforts to be visible and available to the 3,000 plus strong workforce operating on the 44 sites throughout the United Kingdom. One way in which this was achieved was that the weekly board meeting was held at a different site each week. During each board meeting employees working on the host site were given the opportunity to be recognised and rewarded for their individual improvement efforts by sharing their achievements with the board. Following the board meetings the Managing Director and the attending board members (usually the regional managers) would undergo a 'walk-about' so that they were visible and could genuinely listen and respond to the views of the organisation's people.

## Policy and Strategy

The motto of this company was 'work hard / play hard'. One example of how this was supported was when the annual mission and vision sharing event was held. In the main the morning of this event was dedicated to sharing the organisation's Policy and Strategy with the employees and the afternoon dedicated to having fun. Often a well-known comedian would be invited to provide entertainment for the afternoon. During the site visit the assessors verified that most of the employees who could attend the day, did attend the day (even when this involved a long coach journey) because they all really enjoyed the event, whether they were interested in the mission and vision or not.

## People

There was a real feel within the organisation that its people were valued. Appraisal was fully deployed, training and development opportunities maximised and evidence of providing career opportunities within the organisation for staff who wanted them. Managers' performance related pay was aligned to the feedback from the people perception survey, and so if a particular department's people were not happy the manager would not be rewarded financially. Furthermore, recruitment processes ensured that managers were recruited on the basis that they would value the efforts of the organisation's people.

## Partnerships and Resources

There was much evidence of joint problem solving with suppliers and customers of the organisation. Process maps had been prepared and improved upon with a variety of partners. An example relating to resources was in the generic PowerPoint slides that had been prepared for use by any staff giving a presentation on the organisation's performance. This initiative meant everyone had access to the latest information, and duplication in relation to preparing slides was eradicated. Furthermore there was a corporate identity when sharing information with external agencies.

## Processes
Front-line staff provided the assessor team with numerous examples of applying quality tools like process maps, cause and effect diagrams and Pareto analysis to improving processes, which impacted on customers. The organisation had a good understanding of processes in use.

## Customer Results
Perceptions of customers were improving and all the 'key' customers were happy with their named customer care manager. Customer complaints were minimal.

## People Results
84% of the organisation's people completed the people perception survey. When asked about this during the site visit a very clear message emerged. Basically the survey forms were completed because the staff knew that their comments would be acted upon. Motivation amongst the people also showed positive trends because they felt involved and informed with and in the company's progress. Each department had a display board, which contained the organisation's, and each department's main targets and performance in relation to those targets. At first the assessor team thought that these performance boards were created solely for the site visit but it soon became evident that they reflected an ongoing template running through the whole organisation.

## Society Results
The organisation was making some efforts towards minimising their impact on society. An example was the recycling of plastic cups from the staff rooms and using fuel that was associated with less polluting emissions.

## Key Performance Results
The company could demonstrate an impressive 20% increase in market share over the last few years. Consequently, financial performance showed positive trends over the last 5 years.

Finally, the organisation assessed became a finalist and was awarded prize winner status. The assessment team was impressed with this organisation and felt that they should have won.  Particularly as the whole team felt that, for the first time in their lives they had *'stepped out of the real world and walked into a world of quality'*.  The profound event converted the team members from feeling that concepts of the EFQM Excellence Model were really out of reach to recognising that with focused efforts, teamwork and good leadership an organisation can truly demonstrate its achievements towards excellence.

# Chapter 3
# Recognised Implementation Approaches for EFQM Excellence Model

### Characteristics associated with successful implementation

According to writers in the area of implementing total quality management and thereby excellence the characteristics associated with successful implementation are similar to the characteristics of excellence in healthcare. (see Chapter 1). Armed with this information organisations embarking upon such a journey or reviewing progress in their journey towards excellence can use the following information to determine how many of the characteristics are present in their own [planned] approach. By doing this organisations are applying a self-assessment framework with a similar structure to the EFQM Excellence Model to their implementation approach whilst also using the Model to attain excellence.

It could be argued that the EFQM Excellence Model contains all the characteristics below and so a self-assessment in the area of implementation is not required. Whilst this may be the case for the cultural aspects namely, strong leadership, involvement, empowerment, customer focus including an internal customer focus, teamwork, trust (a no blame culture that focuses on system improvements and not people) and organisational commitment for excellence, it is not so explicit for the implementation plan.

For instance, in practice the [planned] implementation approach can often be overlooked when utilising the Model, especially in the area of measuring progress in relation to the original plan. As a consequence the holistic efforts of the organisation towards excellence are compromised which can result in disjointed efforts. In other words, some departments will be using the principles and concepts of excellence extremely well whilst others are not using them at all. It would be this type of scenario that the self-assessment against the original plan would uncover and thereby provide the stimulus to agree corrective actions. When considering which characteristics are required for successful implementation it would be useful to examine the suggested 'actions for successful implementation' and supporting narrative given in this chapter. These have emerged from amalgamating the recommendations from a number of writers in the areas of quality, healthcare quality and changing an organisation's culture. It is by no way a prescriptive list but does provide ideas for agreeing the contents of an implementation plan and for reviewing any approach currently underway.

## Actions for successful implementation

*Set up a steering committee with appropriate representation*

According to Brannan (1998) a Model known as the quality in daily work (QIDW) Model, which was implemented in a Hospital in Wisconsin, United States of America is a perfect example of how to implement total quality management [excellence] effectively. In essence this model breaks down the process of quality planning into six steps, the first being to establish a quality council. Brannan (1998) maintains that the responsibilities of this quality council include forming the infrastructure to support the implementation of excellence; establishing processes and assigning individuals to teams, allocating resources and evaluating, screening and selecting projects.

Collard and Sivyer (1990) also observed that the most effective programmes tended to be those that operated through a steering committee with representatives from each of the major functions. Clearly this committee would need to reflect that the leaders of the organisation are committed to excellence and act in such a way that they actively drive and support the journey towards excellence. Experience also suggests that this committee would more likely attain success if its members were chosen and valued by the chief executive.

*Develop a vision for excellence*

Handy (1985) recognised that *'any effective organisation is going somewhere'*. Consequently, when this view is applied to an implementation plan for using the EFQM Excellence Model it implies that a plan would include a clear vision of what successful implementation looks like. For instance, determining the organisational norms, values and behaviours that the implementation plan would be designed to achieve would be a pre-requisite for a successful culture change process, (Gordon 1987). Building on this concept Brannan (1998) recommends that these norms, values and behaviours should be those that are perceived as important by the organisation's customers. In line with this Brannan (1998) suggests developing quality indicators for the organisation to allow the development of quality goals.

What Brannan (1998) does not make clear though is that *'winning'* organisations are those that focus on both their internal (employees) and external customers. Particularly as they tend to anticipate the changing needs of their customers and have the internal strength and service orientation to meet the customer needs identified. (Azzolini & Shillaber 1993) Hence the vision for excellence should contain clarity around the norms, values and behaviours of an organisation focused on the needs of its internal (employees) and its external customers.

### Develop a strategy for implementation

Øvretveit (1998) believes that quality has never been planned or co-ordinated in national healthcare systems which has meant that healthcare suffers from a proliferation of uncoordinated activities that provide little evidence of effectiveness. This being the case, it would suggest that healthcare personnel have never appreciated the enormity of the challenge inherent within securing a change in culture, (Evenden and Anderson 1992). Neither have they taken on board the recommendation of Megginson et al (1989) who maintain that failing to plan for a change in culture is disastrous.

With regards to the content of the implementation plan, Evenden and Anderson (1992) assert that it needs to ensure people are kept informed about progress, staff are involved in the decisions of how the change is to be implemented and opportunities are highlighted. Furthermore, the implementation plan needs to re-emphasise the organisation's values and carefully consider the timing of events. The latter aspect therefore indicates that prioritising areas for change is interdependent with timing.

In line with this thinking Azzolini and Shillaber (1993) strongly recommend using an orderly process for agreeing value-adding priorities to avoid '*helter-skelter*' improvement activities. Particularly as organisations tend to fall into two major traps, that of failing to set priorities for closing gaps and an incomplete or incorrect analysis of root causes. The implication here is that organisations need to undertake a self-assessment of where they are in relation to excellence prior to determining priorities within the implementation plan. A view supported by Collard and Sivyer (1990) who suggest that it is crucial that an organisation understands where it is in relation to excellence before it embarks upon agreeing the priorities within the action plan.

### Implement strategy (take action)

Taking action to ensure the organisation contains the characteristics of excellence involves a number of activities including:

Visible Chief Executive commitment – Oakland (1989) maintains that leadership commitment needs to be '*obsessional*' if excellence is to be achieved. Furthermore, this commitment needs to be visible as the organisation's people will not respond as hoped unless they receive regular reinforcement that the leaders are applying the concepts of excellence that the employees are expected to apply. Therefore the behaviour of top managers *must* represent the values and expectations of the new culture, (Gordon 1987).

Integration – Øvretveit (1999) maintains that without integration an organisation does not use its resources to best effect. Instead '*We get a technique without heart, and systems without soul which do not heal or enable people to grow.*' Furthermore integrating current activities that reflect the desired values of the organisation enables people to continue working within their '*comfort zone*' whilst gradually taking on board new concepts and new ways of working. So existing meetings and training and development opportunities can be enhanced to support the implementation process rather than discarded for seemingly totally new developments that do not always engender the support that is envisaged.

A launch – Organisations may consider planning a formal launch for using the EFQM Excellence Model depending upon the messages they want to promote. Collard and Sivyer (1990) also observed that successful organisations did not rely on one-off launches but included successive rebirths to regularly boost the drive towards excellence.

Intense education and training – May (1998) commented that her experience had led to the conclusion that everyone involved in quality [excellence] programmes within healthcare had a different idea about what they were doing and why they were doing it. Crosby (1980) also maintains that individuals 'retard' their own intellectual growth, rely on habits and stop learning. Consequently, Crosby (1980) suggests that an implementation programme should include three forms of education, namely, orientation to the concepts and procedures of quality, direct skill improvement and a continual low-level but concentrated barrage of quality idea communications. Wright (1997) supported this approach as he observed that some healthcare professionals diligently applied one of the quality tools without really knowing why. Wright (1997) thereby warned against teaching skills without facilitating the transfer of knowledge, which is often achieved by application and the exposure to repeated messages of the benefits attained from striving for excellence, in addition to the various training and development opportunities.

Phased introduction of the Model concepts – Wright (1997) observed that healthcare professionals tend to feel that little can be learned from other sectors, which means they do not readily accept the learning potential from other organisations. Jackson (2000) observed a similar scenario when applying the EFQM Excellence Model within maternity services. Consequently, a successful implementation approach is associated with a phased introduction of the concepts of the EFQM Excellence Model. (Øvretveit 1999, Jackson 2000)

<u>Expert facilitation</u> – As a result of comparing the quality programmes of six hospitals Øvretveit (1999) found that expert facilitation for project teams and heads of departments was associated with successful implementation. Jackson (2000) also found this to be beneficial if not vital when implementing the EFQM Excellence Model within maternity services. Additionally, experience has shown that facilitators who are *expert* in healthcare as well as excellence are more likely to secure commitment for using the EFQM Excellence Model because they agree a more practical application approach that aligns closely to the values of healthcare professionals.

<u>Good communications</u> – People need to be kept informed of progress relating to the implementation programme (Evenden and Anderson 1992), in order to minimise resistance, (Brannan 1998). Clearly good communications need to be timely and appropriate. Accordingly this would be achieved by utilising a variety of methods including, verbal, written (paper and electronic), display notices, award ceremonies, conferences and other special events and incidences. In addition, these methods need to be used regularly to secure maximum effect. (Brannan 1998)

<u>The use of quality tools</u> – EFQM (1997) recognise that self-assessment alone does not deliver continuous improvement. Rather improvement actions are required. Furthermore, these improvement actions are often facilitated by the use of generic quality tools like Pareto analysis, cause and effective diagrams, process mapping, statistical process control and histograms. It would be expected that the expert facilitator is familiar with these concepts and the training and development opportunities aligned to support their use.

<u>Securing quick successes</u> – Given that achieving the characteristics associated with organisational excellence takes time, it is important to secure early and easy successes. Jackson et al (1998) found this to be the case when implementing the concepts of self-assessment and continuous improvement within the clinical support services of a hospital. Similarly the advice was to prevent over enthusiasm with regards to improvement projects embarked upon, as there is a tendency to '*bite off more than you can chew*', a situation which can have a debilitating effect on progress, (Jackson et al 1998). This demonstrates a major advantage of the EFQM Excellence Model in that it is a non-prescriptive framework, which means the team can prioritise the areas for improvement actions, as opposed to the Model driving the prioritisation process.

<u>Celebrating success</u> – Ensuring that the implementation programme contains a constant barrage of quality idea communications, involves publicising successes

on a regular basis. (Collard and Sivyer 1990)  Furthermore, Brannan (1998) noted that recognising and celebrating successes was an extremely important aspect of the implementation programme for securing ongoing commitment.

Recognising staff – Recognising staff is a very important factor in the implementation programme for excellence. (Brannan 1998)  This can include one to one recognition events (formal or informal), award ceremonies and publication tools directed at organisational and wider audiences.  Outside media may be utilised for recognising the achievements of the organisation's people an approach that engenders pride from the organisation to the employee and conversely from the employee to the organisation.

Having in place a process that ensures everyone is responsible for achieving excellence – Achieving a culture indicative of excellence requires everyone to be involved in the process.  Hence it is up to programme leaders and organisational managers to ensure everyone contributes to the quality [excellence] journey.  Activities that support this include, recognising staff, good communications, appropriate education and training programmes, publicising success and a formal system for reviewing progress.

Committing ongoing resources – The most significant resource that can be deployed towards applying the EFQM Excellence Model into everyday practice is energy, creativity and time.  However, personal experience has also found that information requirements are paramount for success, hence the recommendation to consider the resources required to meet the ongoing and ever expansive information needs of an organisation using the Model to achieve excellence.

*Apply the RADAR logic*
Taylor (1995) maintains that all too often, organisations do not take the time to periodically step back to reflect and assess how the quality [excellence] journey is really going.  Similarly, Azzolini and Shillaber (1993) assert that interim progress reviews are needed to ensure that action plans remain realistic and are continuously improved. It can therefore be argued that because the EFQM Excellence Model is based on continuous improvement it is an ideal tool for reviewing progress.  Hence, should the EFQM Excellence Model self-assessment framework be applied to the implementation approach it would mean that the RADAR logic would need to be used in order to determine the strengths and areas for improvement of the approach.  As a result, corrective actions to address the areas for improvement could be agreed and put into effect thereby facilitating successful implementation of the EFQM Excellence Model into healthcare practice.

Failure to plan for using the self-assessment technique on the implementation approach suggests that this important aspect of achieving excellence will never be put into practice. Especially, as it is recognised that often failure to plan means that it probably will never happen. (Azzolini & Shillaber 1993) Although, the effort required for doing this cannot be underestimated.

Nevertheless, change is never easy and has to be achieved one step at a time, (Azzolini & Shillaber 1993). Given this to be the case it may be useful and reassuring to note that it is the direction of the organisation rather than its speed, that is important in the journey towards excellence.

## Implementation approaches supported by EFQM

There is no one best way of implementing the EFQM Excellence Model into all organisations, (Dale et al 1994). In view of this the European Foundation for Quality Management suggests a number of approaches for implementing the use of the EFQM Excellence Model, which are questionnaire, matrix chart, workshop, proforma and award simulation.

The EFQM (1999) recognise that each implementation approach delivers different benefits and involves different resources and risks. Before an approach is chosen it is important to consider what the organisation is hoping to achieve by using the Model. For instance, if the aim is to secure a 'quick fix' to a specific problem then this is unlikely to occur given the long-term nature of the Model. Alternatively, if the organisation is looking to achieve a quality award it must be remembered that the RADAR scoring matrix awards higher scores to organisations who can demonstrate positive trends for more than 5 years, in a wide scope of result areas. This implies that continuous improvement efforts needed to have been well underway prior to embarking upon the EFQM Excellence Model for attaining an award.

In line with this thinking the EFQM (1999) suggest the type of approaches that are suitable for organisations who are well on the way with applying quality concepts and frameworks in addition to those that are just starting the journey. A distinction is also made between the amount of effort required for each approach in terms of low, medium and high effort. Clearly these choices depend upon the availability of resources within the organisation regarding commitment, time, energy, information and finance. Likewise, the organisation may consider applying the Model throughout all departments at once or design a phased approach, whereby some departments will apply it before others, dependent upon the aforementioned resources available.

Irrespective of the approach chosen EFQM (1999) suggests there are eight main steps for carrying out a self-assessment with the EFQM Excellence Model. See Figure 3.1

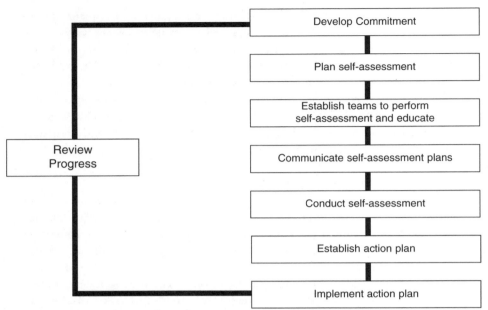

**Figure 3.1 Eight main steps for applying the EFQM Excellence Model within healthcare (EFQM 1999)**

The eight steps are not necessarily linear as some activities may be undertaken simultaneous to each other. What is important is that the organisation must not lose sight of why they are using the Model.

Only a brief explanation will be given regarding each approach as more information can be obtained from contacting the EFQM and requesting a copy of their publication 'Assessing for Excellence. A Practical guide for Self-Assessment'. (EFQM 1999b)

*Questionnaire approach*
Deemed by the EFQM (1999) as one of the least labour intensive approaches (providing an existing questionnaire is used) the questionnaire self-assessment approach aims to obtain the views of [all] the people within the organisation. The benefits associated with this approach are that it is quick and easy to apply, can involve all the organisation's people, supports communication efforts and can be used in conjunction with other approaches. (EFQM 1999)

The associated risks are that the strengths and areas for improvement cannot be ascertained, accuracy of feedback is dependent upon the phrasing of the original questions, there may be questionnaire fatigue within the organisation and expectations can be raised and unfulfilled if timely, appropriate actions do not occur. (EFQM 1999)

*Matrix chart approach*

In essence the matrix chart approach requires an organisation to create a series of achievement statements that can be assigned a rating from 1-10. Statements would have to be identified for all the nine criteria of the Model, thereby involving the creation of 90 achievement statements in total. The matrix chart is then used by management teams who self-assess where the organisation is in relation to the statements. To clarify extracts from the Leadership element of the matrix chart, found within the EFQM Practical Guide (1999), are given below.

Statement with a rate of 1 – The MIS (Management Information Services) management team has a process in place to develop its own awareness of the concepts of Total Quality.

Statement with a rate of 4 – Leaders act as role models for MIS' values and expectations, and regularly review their own effectiveness as leaders.

Statement with a rate of 7 – The MIS management team is proactive in valuing, recognising and rewarding all employees for continuous improvement.

Statement with a rate of 10 – The MIS management team is proactive in promoting creativity, new ideas and motivation in order to sustain continuous improvement and to foster a culture of Customer Focus, (EFQM 1999).

The benefits associated with this approach are that it is simple to use, requires minimal training, can involve all the organisation's people, supports team discussion and clearly demonstrates progress and the lack of progress in relation to all the nine criteria, (EFQM 1999).

The associated risks are that the list of strengths and areas for improvement are not produced, it does not allow comparisons against EQA applicants and there is no direct cross reference between the matrix statements and the sub-criteria of the Model, (EFQM 1999).

*Workshop approach*

The workshop approach has five distinct phases training, data collection, a scoring workshop, prioritisation of improvement actions and a review of progress that becomes part of the normal review process for the organisation. The benefits associated with this approach are that it; is an excellent way to familiarise management teams to understand the Model, supports team building, allows for discussion and agreement regarding the strengths and areas for improvement which provides motivation towards improvement actions, (EFQM 1999).

The associated risks are that it is less robust than the award simulation approach, requires expert facilitation and can result in unrealistic, often over generous scoring, (EFQM 1999).

*Pro-forma approach*

The pro-forma approach involves using of a set of pro-formas, which in total contain all the 32 sub-criteria of the EFQM Excellence Model. Figure 3.2 contains extracts from the example given in the EFQM booklet 'Assessing for Excellence. A Practical Guide for Self-Assessment'. (EFQM 1999)

---

## Criterion 1

### Leadership

How leaders develop and facilitate the achievement of the mission and vision, develop values required for long term success and implement these via appropriate actions and behaviours, and are personally involved in ensuring the organisation's management system is developed and implemented.

### Sub-criterion 1a

Leaders develop the mission, vision and values and are role models of a culture of Excellence.

**Areas to address**

How leaders:
- develop and role model ethics and values which support the creation of the organisation's culture
- are personally and actively involved in improvement activities
- review and improve the effectiveness of their own leadership and act upon future leadership requirements
- stimulate and encourage collaboration within the organisation

**Strengths**
- The senior management team has developed a management competencies model that supports the organisation's values
- Effectiveness of leaders is assessed by employee survey and 360 degree appraisals

**Areas for improvement**
- Leaders are not personally involved in improvement activities

**Evidence**
- Competencies model available on organisation's intranet

- Staff survey data from surveys of 1994, 1996 and 1998 appropriately segmented and individual leader's improvement actions included in their appraisement process

| Approach | Deployment | Assessment & Review | Overall Score |
|---|---|---|---|
| 60% | 50% | 20% | 45% |

---

**Figure 3.2  Extracts from example given in EFQM booklet 'Assessing for Excellence. A Practical Guide for Self-Assessment'. (EFQM 1999)**

Assessment teams collect the appropriate information and then use the pro-formas to undertake a self-assessment. The benefits associated with this approach are that it provides factual information, delivers a list of strengths and areas for improvement, can involve a range of the organisation's people and provides a reasonably accurate indication of an award application score. (EFQM 1999)

The associated risks are that; the process is dependent upon good data collection and the pro-formas can stifle recognition of the full story relating to excellence development. (EFQM 1999)

*Award simulation approach*

The award simulation approach is in essence a replication of the process for entering for the European Quality Award. It involves preparing a full submission document abiding by the criteria laid down in the EFQM Award Application brochure, (EFQM 2000). Subsequently a team of trained assessors, either internal or external to the organisation, scores the application and provides a feedback report containing a list of strengths and areas for improvement.

The benefits associated with this approach are that it provides a list of strengths and areas for improvement, an excellent communication document, an opportunity to compare performance with other organisations and a rehearsal for applying for the EQA. The associated risks are less involvement of managers because the task is usually delegated, a potential for creative writing and it can be too ambitious for an organisation early on in its journey towards excellence. (EFQM 1999)

## The do's and don'ts of implementation

The following do's and don'ts regarding the implementation of the EFQM Excellence Model into healthcare practice come from personal experience and from the advice given by John Øvretveit (1999) after he compared six hospitals integrating quality concepts.

## The recommended do's of implementation

*Plan the process before you start*

It is always useful to have some idea of how you want to apply the concepts of the EFQM Excellence Model. If you are new to using the Model within healthcare then it may be wise not to use the whole framework at once thereby implying that you may not want to use any of the approaches recommended by the EFQM. Instead you may prefer to develop your own, based on the information provided in this Chapter and/or that in Chapter 4 where the achievements associated with applying the Model in a number of healthcare environments and in a variety of ways is discussed.

Imperative for identifying a preferred implementation approach is to determine the reason behind using the Model. In other words, what are the intended gains and outcomes that the organisation is hoping to realise. Once this has been agreed an appropriate process for implementation can be planned. Clearly the plan will differ for organisations wanting to apply for the European Quality Award (EQA) and for those who do not.

*Sell the concepts over the specifics of the Model*
The specifics of the Model are the nine criteria (Leadership, Policy and Strategy, People, Partnerships and Resources, Processes, Customer Results, People Results, Society Results and Key Performance Results) and the sub-criteria questions. The concepts of the Model include:
- customer focus;
- results orientation;
- people involvement;
- continuous improvement;
- innovation and learning.

Therefore it is more important that the organisation's people feel valued and energised to make customer focused improvements than it is that they can recite the specific sub-criteria of the EFQM Excellence Model. Consequently, the way that the organisation intends to achieve this needs to be considered during the planning process. In particular, plans need to contain details regarding communication and training and development opportunities that will be provided regarding the use of the EFQM Excellence Model.

*Start simple*
Irrespective of the comprehensive nature of the Model, there is no need to apply it in its total form initially. Especially, if the aim is to secure continuous improvement (focusing on the concepts) rather than apply for the EQA. Furthermore, applying the whole Model can be off-putting to the novice and detract from the main objective of improving healthcare. Hence, the advice to start simple which can secure tangible and motivational benefits for the organisation is sound.

*Integrate the EFQM Excellence Model*
It is far better to apply the RADAR principle to your current way of working than to see the EFQM Excellence Model as an 'add-on'. Healthcare personnel are too busy to take on initiatives that do not align to their values for

delivering better care for patients and securing a better work environment for the organisation's people. This in mind, a useful integration approach in the first instance is to apply the RADAR logic to existing initiatives as often elements of RADAR are found to be missing from current improvement activities. In other words, experience has found that many initiatives fail to determine the desired results, measure actual deployment and undertake assessment and review, a situation that does need to be addressed in the interests of providing better healthcare.

*Allow everyone to be involved and experience the learning curve*
The EFQM Excellence Model subscribes to the principle that team working is a better approach when striving for continuous improvement. Therefore the more people that can be involved the better. However, different people learn at different rates and often need different experiences to reach the understanding necessary to see the value of using the Model in healthcare. Recognising this, being sensitive to it and creative in achieving total involvement will help any organisation in its journey towards excellence.

*Retain a high level of visible commitment and drive*
Leaders within the organisation need to make their continuous improvement efforts very visible if they want others to be committed to the same values. People are much happier when they are following a good example and role model. However, retaining a high level of visible commitment and drive can be challenging at times, so the drivers of excellence may need to identify a support group or key people who help continue their efforts through difficult, challenging and questionable times. During a recent quality in healthcare conference, a dentist from Switzerland expressed from the heart that *'he who strives for quality lives in a lonely flat'*; sometimes it feels like a lonely planet but that does not mean despondency has a place in the pursuit of excellence. Instead the driver of excellence needs to identify strategies that will help him/her manage such challenges. A suggestion would be to attend a regular conference like the European Forum for Quality Improvement in Healthcare organised by the British Medical Association in London, it is very inspiring and exposes the leader to excellent networking opportunities with like minded people.

**Summary Box: Do's and Dont's of Implementation**

| Do's | Dont's |
|------|--------|
| • plan the process between your staff | • let it be an audit or another paper exercise |
| • sell the concepts over the specifics of the Model | • get hung up on fitting initiatives neatly into a criterion |
| • start simple | • spend time identifying why the concept cannot be applied |
| • integrate the EFQM Excellence Model | • let your enthusiasm wane |
| • allow everyone to be involved and experience the learning curve | • have a rigid plan for implementation |
| • retain a high level of visible commitment and drive | |

## The recommended don'ts of implementation

*Let it be an audit or another paper exercise*

In practice, audit tends to be a 'one-off' activity rather than a normal day to day way of working. Furthermore, audits are often undertaken against a set of standards, which have a fixed end point. In contrast, the EFQM Excellence Model is an everyday management framework designed to support continuous improvement. So efforts need to be deployed to prevent the Excellence Model being used as a 'one-off' data collection exercise thereby implying that the process needs to be cyclic in terms of information gathering in addition to being action oriented when securing continuous improvements for healthcare.

If an organisation or a department find themselves spending more time on completing paper work than on making healthcare improvements (for patients and staff) then they are not using the Model correctly. Avoiding a paper exercise is challenging but has to be effected if ongoing, actual improvements are to be the normal way of working. Learning from others is a useful endeavour for dealing with this.

*Get hung up on fitting initiatives neatly into a criterion*
Not all of healthcare enablers and results fit neatly into the sub-criteria of the EFQM Excellence Model. Therefore time should not be wasted trying to make them do that. Instead if an enabler or result has been identified which is worthy of applying the RADAR concept to then it should be accommodated into sub-criteria agreed by the team as quickly as possible. Once the enabler or result has been accommodated time can be spent undertaking the self-assessment, putting in place improvement actions and learning more about the Model. There is nothing to stop any team in any organisation from transferring an item from one sub-criterion to another, at any stage of the process. Indeed seeing this as a normal course of events at the outset aligns well to the reality that people within the organisation learn at different rates and through different stimuli. Thereby implying that some enablers and/or results will be self-assessed within less appropriate sub-criteria initially than later on in the journey.

*Spend time identifying reasons why the concept cannot be applied*
The concept of making continuous improvements for the benefits of patients, staff and other key stakeholders is one that all healthcare people are signed up to. So it would seem inappropriate to identify reasons why the concept should not be applied once the leaders within the organisation have decided to utilise the EFQM Excellence Model to support the journey towards continuous improvement. A better approach would be to explore creative ways to integrate the initiative into current activities thereby applying the principles of the Model more effectively.

*Let your enthusiasm wane*
There is no doubt that securing improvements in healthcare is an energetic process, which can be very difficult at times. It is therefore important that everyone, especially the leaders within the organisation ensure that their enthusiasm does not wane. Similar strategies identified for maintaining a high level of visible commitment can be used here.

*Have a rigid plan for implementation*
It is far better to have the support of the team than to follow a strict implementation plan. Therefore any plan which has been prepared should be on the understanding that it may have to be amended in light of the reality of implementing it. Jackson (2000) found that minor amendments needed to be made to the overall plan for maternity services which in turn proved more successful than if the original plan and proposed timings had been adhered to. A factor which supports not having a rigid plan for implementation is the observation by Taylor (1995) whereby most success with quality programmes

were achieved when off the shelf packages for implementation had been avoided.

Instead desired achievements are more likely to be recognised when organisations carefully evolve and mould their own implementation package which is context specific and focused on the particular customer needs relating to that industry. It is for this reason that implementation approaches used within healthcare are the subject of the next chapter.

# Chapter 4
# Implementing the EFQM Excellence Model within Healthcare

## Public and voluntary sectors version of the EFQM Excellence Model

Initially self-assessment Models were created for profit centred organisations that needed to thrive in a competitive market place. More recently however, there has been a growing demand for public and voluntary sector organisations to use the EFQM Excellence Model framework to respond to the changing demands within their environment. In response to the growing demand, EFQM (1999) produced a Public and Voluntary Sectors version of the Excellence Model.

In comparison to the core Model there are only a small number of changes in the Public and Voluntary Sectors version of Model, which are mostly found in the *'areas to address'*. The changes reflect a number of characteristics associated with public and not-for-profit sector organisations. These include the interface between managerial and political roles, the situation that customers are not necessarily primary users of the service, the restrictions placed on organisations by governments and legislation, and on financial constraints, (EFQM 1999).

Nevertheless there are still some areas to address that require interpretation. An example being in Key Performance Indicators (9b) that contains 'time to market' in the processes' section. When healthcare personnel are asked to relate this to their field of practice, they often experience difficulty. However, when a little lateral thinking is applied it is easy to see that 'time to market' can be interpreted as 'time to implement research into practice' (managerial or clinical). It stands to reason that shortening this time reflects a desirable continuous improvement and is also an area of concern for healthcare. Likewise in the Performance Indicators of the Customer Results criterion there is an area to address that contains the text 'defect, error and rejection rates' in the products and services section. Clearly this could relate to, number of times a patient was sent the wrong appointment details, or failed to attend for an outpatient appointment.

With regards to interpreting an enabler, sub-criterion 2a (Policy and Strategy are based on the present and future needs and expectations of stakeholders) contains the area to address *gathering and understanding information to define the market and market segment the organisation will operate in both now and in the future*. Whilst at first glance the area to address may appear to have no relevance to healthcare, it can soon be seen that this statement readily applies to gathering and understanding demographic data from which current and future services are prioritised by healthcare organisations. Interpreting the Model terminology is one of the major contributions of an expert facilitator when supporting a healthcare organisation to apply the EFQM Excellence Model.

There are many other examples than those given above, which can help to promote understanding and the use of the Public and Voluntary Sectors version of the EFQM Excellence Model within healthcare. Some of which can be found in the articles by Jackson (1999 and 2000), whereby the alignment between government healthcare policy and the EFQM Excellence Model is explored.

### Suitability of the EFQM Excellence Model within Healthcare

There are a number of UK government guidelines and directives, which can be delivered via the EFQM Excellence Model. To illustrate, when the fundamental principles of the EFQM Excellence Model are compared to the core principles of The NHS Plan (Department of Health 2000), it can be seen that there is much alignment. (See Table 4.1)

Further similarities have been found with the governmental approach to controls assurance. For instance, the UK Government maintained that achieving objectives and controlling risks is dependent upon the process of self-assessment (NHS Executive 1999a), the same approach utilised by the EFQM Excellence Model. Similarly it was recommended that clinical governance should start with a baseline assessment of the organisation's position, (NHS Executive 1999a).

Moreover, the Government recognised that it would take at least ten years to attain a culture reflective of the many characteristics of quality [excellence]. Likewise, the EFQM recognise that securing a quality culture takes time as organisations need to demonstrate 5years of continuous improvement before they can be deemed as having excellence status.

| Example of some of the core principles of the NHS Plan (Department of Health 2000) | Example of some of the fundamental principles of the EFQM Excellence Model (EFQM 1999) |
|---|---|
| The NHS will shape its services around the needs and preferences of individual patients, their families and their carers | The customer is the final arbiter of product and service quality and customer loyalty, retention and market share is best optimised through clear focus on the needs of current and potential customers |
| The NHS will respond to different needs of different populations | |
| The NHS will work continuously to improve quality of services and to minimise errors | Organisations perform more effectively when all inter-related activities are understood and planned improvements are made |
| The NHS will support and value its staff | The full potential of an organisation's people is best released through shared values and a culture of trust and empowerment, which encourages the involvement of everyone |
| The NHS will work together with others to ensure a seamless service for patients | An organisation works more effectively when it has mutually beneficial relationships, built on trust, sharing of knowledge and integration, with its partners |

**Table 4.1   Alignment of some of the core principles of the NHS Plan with some of the fundamental principles of the EFQM Excellence Model**

A final example given here relates to a statement from the Department of Health that noted that the expectations laid upon NHS Trusts were so challenging that they required good leadership, and that a quality organisation would ensure that leadership skills were developed. (DoH 1997)  The EFQM Excellence Model is based on the premise that *'Excellent results with respect to Performance, Customers, People and Society are achieved through* LEADERSHIP *driving Policy and Strategy, People, Partnerships and Resources and Processes'*,(EFQM 1999).   Furthermore, the process of self-assessment and continuous improvement needs to be applied to the performance of the organisation's leaders, in order that good leadership is developed, reviewed and meeting the demands of excellence.  For more information in this area see the article by Jackson (1999).

Other well known approaches that can be delivered via the EFQM Excellence Model are Investors in People, accreditation by professional Royal Colleges dealing with complaints, and accreditation using the International Standards Organisation (ISO) framework. Despite such ideal alignment, there are specific challenges within healthcare regarding the use of the EFQM Excellence Model.

**Implementation challenges within healthcare**
The characteristics associated with successful implementation of the concepts of excellence include good leadership, teamwork, a no blame culture, good communications, skills in relation to quality concepts and tools, empowerment, creativity, a results orientation, good information systems and a drive for continuous improvement. However, these characteristics are lacking in healthcare as the following information demonstrates.

*Good leadership*
As yet there is little evidence that good leadership is a common feature of the NHS. An indication of this can be gleaned from the comment of a panel of experts during a seminar on professional and managerial cultures within the

NHS who maintained that a 'top-down' approach to objective setting was not enough, rather '*leaders needed to be in place at all levels*' (Agnew 2000). Similarly, Maynard (2000) purported that nursing required much needed improvements in its leadership and Barbara Stocking, a Regional Director was quoted as saying '*The NHS is desperately short of leaders at local level*', (McIntosh et al 2000), Furthermore, the Department of Health has set up a working group to look at the skills required of good NHS leaders, which likewise confirms there is a lack of good leadership in the NHS.

### Teamwork

A further theme during the seminar on professional and managerial cultures within the NHS was the divide between managers and clinicians (Agnew 2000), which strongly indicated the absence of a teamwork culture. Again this is not something that hasn't been previously recognised, as a lack of teamwork is a significant emerging factor in the work relating to the development of integrated care pathways.

### No blame culture

A no-blame culture means that improvements will be primarily directed at systems rather than individuals. However, the NHS is noted as having a <u>blame</u> culture (Baker 2000), rather than a no-blame culture, from which symptoms often become public.

### Good communications

Wakeley (1997) expressed concern regarding the potential for poor communications within a healthcare organisation and the wider healthcare environment, which personal experience would suggest is a real concern.

### Relevant skills

During the 2000 NHS Confederation Conference, Barbara Stocking suggested that people with the relevant skills for change were not available to the NHS (McIntosh et al 2000). Furthermore, this does not appear to be a new problem as Wilson et al (1999), maintained that successful change was an unlikely occurrence unless key staff were in place with the necessary skills and knowledge to lead and apply quality initiatives.

### Empowerment and Creativity

Empowerment would also seem to be lacking in healthcare as Ken Jarrold, a Health Authority Chief Executive thought he was doing leaders a favour when he suggested that '*We must give the senior people in our healthcare system 'do-able' jobs*'. If 'We' must allocate jobs then this in itself confirms that there is no scope for empowerment or creativity.

### Results orientation

Within healthcare there is a tendency to measure elements of a process rather than the outcomes whether they be desired or achieved, (Eaton 2000). Furthermore, this tendency to measure process is ingrained into healthcare personnel who experience real difficulty when asked to determine the desired results for their area of practice. Personal experience has found this to be the case irrespective of whether the healthcare employee works within a clinical or a non-clinical environment. Failure to determine the desired results implies that healthcare does not have a clear direction and so therefore cannot be focusing its efforts towards excellence.

### Good information systems

Once the desired results have been identified the need for sound information systems become paramount. However, good information systems are not a common feature within healthcare, and in some cases 'there is an awful long way to go', (McIntosh 1998).

### Continuous improvement

Inherent within a culture that subscribes to continuous improvement is that priorities are clear and the journey planned. In contrast, this is not the case for healthcare as bolt-on, knee-jerk reactions to hot issues of the day are a more normal aspect of everyday practice, (Ainsworth 2000). Secondly, healthcare personnel are more used to an environment whereby standards are the norm rather than the concept of continuous improvement, a feature that is demonstrated in the following quote.

> *'There is a risk that a performance indicator is chosen because it is easily measured and relates to current processes in which data is recorded rather than because it has validity. Whatever indicators are chosen should conform to defined standards'*, (Myers 1999).

Hence, it can be assumed that implementing the EFQM Excellence Model within a healthcare environment is specifically challenging given that many characteristics associated with a culture of excellence are lacking. Nevertheless, the EFQM Excellence Model has been successfully applied into a number of healthcare organisations not only in the UK but also Europe-wide.

## Overview of deployment within healthcare

In an effort to improve the usage of the Excellence Model within the Public Sector, the EFQM set up working groups for healthcare, education and uniformed services during the year of 1998. The healthcare group has become so successful now that it hosts a minimum of four meetings per year in a different European country each time, where it also provides a formal one-day conference, often supported by the relevant Minister for health or other senior official. (See EFQM website).

During one of the EFQM Health Sector meetings the members tabled information regarding the deployment of the EFQM Excellence Model within their own country's healthcare organisations. The minutes of the June 1999 meeting noted that deployment of the EFQM Excellence Model within healthcare was as follows:

*Austria* – Some early attempts to use the Model, there is University research into total quality management (TQM) methods, hospitals are required to use quality management methods of which ISO is dominant and there is little support from government.

*Belgium* – There is no formal institutional decision on use of the model, although there is some activity by institutions and a network is in existence based on Vlerick Management School.

*Germany* – There is interest in quality assurance and external control mechanisms such as EFQM. There is low level usage of the Model but interest is growing, hospitals are required to appoint a Quality Manager and the Federal Ministry for Health is showing interest in TQM and using 30 hospitals in a pilot.

*Israel* – The EFQM Excellence Model has not arrived yet but there is some knowledge amongst healthcare personnel of the Malcolm Baldridge National Quality Award (MBNQA) self-assessment Model.

*Norway* – Several hospitals are working with the Model, TQM concepts are applied in most hospitals and there is legislation supporting quality councils in each hospital.

*Portugal* – There is support from the government for TQM related activities, there is limited use of the EFQM Excellence Model as a simple diagnostic tool in hospitals and healthcare centres and a partnership is in existence with the Portuguese Association for Quality.

*Spain* – Several regions are using the Model, in the Basque region 100% of the hospitals are using the Model. There is use of quality standards and the EFQM model in some other hospitals. The use of ISO as a basis for implementing quality systems is growing, quality assurance is required by law, and education and training on the use of TQM and the EFQM Excellence Model is provided for healthcare professionals by a University in Madrid.

*Sweden* – A full national survey has been carried out on the use of quality systems (results were not available). There is legislation on systematic continuous improvement, regulatory systems based on TQM and ISO 9004 are being used and some organisations are using the MBNQA self-assessment

Model. There is a Quality Development Leadership system based on Baldridge used in 30% of hospitals and there has been a national quality award since 1996.

*The Netherlands* – 50% (120) of the hospitals know of the Model, 20% are using the Model, six seriously. 30% of mental health care centres are using the Model, it is used in the merging of institutions and the Instituut Nederlandse Kwaliteit has developed a health care specific model based on EFQM.

*Turkey* – There is little government support, ISO 9000 series and TQM is supported in the military hospitals and several University hospitals have ISO 9000 accreditation. Some hospitals and clinics are showing an interest in the Model and several congresses have been planned and held on applying TQM in healthcare.

*United Kingdom* – There is significant interest in applying the Model following the national initiative on clinical governance. 80% of hospitals are engaged in some type of quality activity using Models like Investors in People, Charter Mark and ISO. The chief executive of the NHS supports the use of the Model within healthcare (as documented in the June 1999 minutes). The national health care curriculum will have the Model included, the British Quality Foundation has set up a healthcare common interest group and British Telecom are supporting a pilot competition based on the Model and its use to improve patient care.

Two further reports were tabled during a subsequent meeting of the EFQM Health Sector Group, which provided information regarding deployment with Ireland and Switzerland.

*Ireland* – 25% of hospitals have formal quality programmes in place, 13% have no intention of introducing such programmes, 32% did not know if they would introduce such a programme and 53% did intend introducing a quality programme in the near future. The quality tools quoted as being used included TQM, ISO, Business Process Re-engineering and standard setting. No organisation within the study was using the EFQM Excellence Model. 63% had involved management consultants of which 19% had retained their services.

*Switzerland* - There is no homogeneous approach to quality management or quality assurance. Federal legislation was agreed to integrate all existing approaches. Three years previously a few cantons of Switzerland ordered hospitals to adopt an approach organised by a private quality society and some bigger hospitals chose to adopt this approach. As yet this approach has not

To date no further reports have been submitted to the members of the EFQM Health Sector Group. For more information regarding the activities and membership of the group you can contact the Secretary Henry Stahr at the Centre for Excellence Development, University of Salford, Maxwell Building, Salford, M5 4WT. Tel:+44 (0)161 295 3278.

been reviewed. Hospitals not using a recommended approach had to utilise a minimal data set for reporting to the national hospital association and the national health insurance association. Only a few institutions have chosen the EFQM approach.

The above summary of deployment indicates that there is as yet patchy use of the EFQM Excellence Model within healthcare for which interest is growing rapidly. Even so, despite all the above organisations being in the business of healthcare no one implementation approach has been used. In an effort to demonstrate this, a summary of the variety of approaches used within UK healthcare organisations is provided.

## Successful Implementation approaches used with healthcare

A number of implementation approaches are described using an 'Implementation Framework' that has been developed from the characteristics associated with successful implementation discussed in chapter 3. The information relating to the healthcare organisations singled out for analysis against the 'Implementation Framework' has come from published text and personal knowledge regarding them. The analysis subsequently informs the section that is headed 'Characteristics associated with successful implementation within healthcare'.

## Salford Hospitals NHS Trust

Details obtained from Stahr et al (2000).

*TQM Maturity*
In 1993 the Trust developed an approach for total quality management which built on the previous quality efforts of audit, quality cycle, TQM and resource management. It was named Health Care Quality Management. The Trust used quality tools and techniques since 1994. In February 1995, the Trust formally agreed to use the EFQM Excellence Model.

*Set up a steering committee with appropriate representation*
A Health Care Quality Management Team was set up to support the journey towards excellence. More recently this team has become known as the Excellence Development team which is afforded total support by the Chief Executive.

*Develop a vision for excellence*
The Model was chosen to provide a framework for continuously improving approaches to clinical and non-clinical management. The Trust also defined quality. Once aware of the EFQM Excellence Model the aim was to attain the European Quality Award by 1996. Clearly this was unrealistic.

*Develop a strategy for implementation*
A strategy was developed that included training and development, phasing the usage of the Model within the organisation starting with senior management first then integrating everyday processes into the EFQM Excellence Model framework. The training strategy indicated that a series of short training sessions, followed by coaching and facilitation in the field, followed by reflections on learning and further training on a just-in-time basis was the chosen approach.

*Implement strategy*

Visible Chief Executive Commitment
The Chief Executive's commitment and leadership has been particularly visible and consistent throughout the whole process. Activities demonstrating commitment are attendance at each Chief Executive review and Trust Quality Award ceremonies and personally recognising the efforts of the organisation's people. The Chief Executive actively encouraged the top team of Directors to become more widely involved in the six monthly review process.

Integration
The plan was to slowly integrate the Model into everyday practice, starting with the most senior management level. Three months into implementation guidance on how the self-assessments would form the basis of the performance management of the Trust was issued. Departmental self-assessments and subsequent action plans were integrated into performance managers' performance review meetings. The ongoing cycle of Chief Executive reviews was introduced in 1996 and by the year later the Trust's Strategic Direction and Business Plans and other relevant documents were considered during departmental self-assessments. In 1999, the Trust's management structure was updated to reflect the Model concepts. Government directives like clinical governance and controls assurance were accommodated into the Model framework. By 2000, the EFQM Excellence Model concepts were deeply embedded into the organisation.

Launch
No evidence of a launch found.

Intense education and training
The internal facilitators received the EFQM licensed assessor training. During 1994, training and development opportunities were extended to other key people within the organisation. Training was also provided in the use of

generic quality tools, problem solving techniques and teamwork. The intensity of the training increased from 1995. Opportunities for sharing learning were developed and practised.

Phased introduction of the Model concepts
Initially all the Model concepts were utilised amongst the 'top' team. For the rest of the people within the organisation, a phased approach to using the Model concepts was introduced. By 1997/8 the organisation's people were expressing a readiness to apply the whole of the Model concepts.

Expert facilitation
A member of the Trust's quality team and a PhD student from the local University were trained to provide the expert facilitation.

Good communications
Good communications centred on guidance regarding integration to the relevant personnel only. The message that any weaknesses identified by the teams were to be considered as opportunities for improvement, thereby supporting a no blame culture, was strongly communicated.

The use of quality tools
Generic quality tools were used in addition to the Model. The recommended elements of good project team management (Øvretveit 1999) were practised.

Securing quick successes
Rehabilitation services trained all the staff within the department and involved them in the self-assessments. As a result of using the Model a people survey was carried out within Rehabilitation services and subsequent action taken which saw a significant improvement in staff satisfaction.

Celebrating success
Winners of the quality awards were made public to all employees within the Trust. At the end of each cycle of Chief Executive reviews best practice was/is shared and success celebrated. Over 160 significant improvements to the service have been demonstrated since using the Model.

Recognising staff
A Quality Award process was introduced which recognised the efforts of improvement teams. Positive feedback to the teams followed each Chief Executive review.

Having in place a process that ensures everyone is responsible for achieving excellence

Initially take up of the Model was not consistent throughout the organisation. Later a formal Chief Executive review process was initiated to facilitate everyone contributing to the journey of excellence. The effort to involve all staff was showing no signs of weakening, (Stahr et al 2000).

Committing ongoing resources

Significant training and development resources were directed towards using the EFQM Excellence Model. Time to develop supportive documentation, undertake self-assessment, corrective action and undergo a six monthly Chief Executive review cycle was committed to the process. Throughout the process the Trust had an Excellence Development Director and more recently appointed an Excellence Development facilitator. Resources to develop information systems have been continually committed.

## Apply RADAR logic to implementation strategy

Stahr et al (2000) provides evidence of RADAR being applied to the implementation strategy from which a number of continuous improvement actions were undertaken.

## Other factors observed

Information systems – An initial review of the self-assessments demonstrated that information systems were poorly orientated to the needs of clinicians and managers.

Learning points – Using the Model demonstrated that some people had difficulty in understanding the difference between results and enablers. In addition, a significant number struggled with defining indicators of performance and some were uncomfortable with the performance being made visible. The need for increasing amounts of training in basic managerial skills such as clarifying results, determining key processes, communication, change management, action planning and implementation of improvement action through teams became evident.

The central importance of the Chief Executive reviews for motivating, coaching and learning emerged.

Using the EFQM Excellence Model provided a framework for clarifying and focusing energies on the organisation's objectives.

The best self-assessments took the form of action learning groups led by a senior clinician or manager.

Consultant medical staff were seen as key because they led the treatment process and determined its priorities. They were also recognised as the most stable members of the workforce and therefore their involvement in continuous improvements viewed as more long-term in comparison to managers.

Integration - The most effective users of the Model consulted 'their' staff over the content of the self-assessment and managed to ensure that the team's self-assessments became part of the business planning process. Of particular importance was the early integration of the EFQM process into the normal management processes rather than being parallel to them.

## South Tees Acute Hospitals NHS Trust
Details obtained from Stahr et al (2000).

*TQM Maturity*
The TQM journey commenced in 1980 with the use of generic quality tools. The organisation attained external recognition by being chosen as a national demonstration site for TQM. By 1990, no less than ten years later, the cultural characteristics associated with an organisation committed to quality were evident. STAHT later developed the core values for the organisation, which were implemented with some degree of success. However, an overarching framework was required that would simultaneously sustain performance and the quality of service delivery.

*Set up a steering committee with appropriate representation*
STAHT developed an Excellence Steering Group, of which the chief executive was an active member from the outset. The overall membership of the group consisted of the Directors, some senior medics and some senior managers of clinical and non-clinical areas. The group had 20 members in total. The remit of the group was to agree priorities for the corporate improvement activities, agree funding allocation for the improvement actions, monitor and review progress on a regular basis, undertake a review of the overall approach and plan the following year's agenda. The membership of the group was also reviewed.

In addition to the corporate steering group, steering groups were set up for staff satisfaction, business results, customer satisfaction and leadership.

*Develop a vision for excellence*
Clarity around the meaning of excellence was agreed following which the Director of Personnel and the leader for Developing Excellence provided a series of workshops in order to share the vision.

When the organisation had travelled some of the journey they determined organisational characteristics from which behaviour profiles emerged particularly in the aspect of leadership.

*Develop a strategy for implementation*
The strategy for implementation contained the following discrete steps; select self-assessment team, educate and train self-assessment team, assign specific tasks to each assessor, conduct self-assessment, agree immediate action plan and set up improvement teams to implement the action plan. It is interesting to note here that at this stage (1995), a review of the whole process was not part of the action plan, nevertheless it was undertaken.

*Implement strategy*
Visible Chief Executive Commitment
It was the Chief Executive who first became interested in the EFQM Excellence Model.

Integration
Full integration has yet to be achieved as at the time of publication the organisation had planned that each division and directorate would use the EFQM Excellence Model as the framework for producing business plans.

Launch
No evidence of a launch could be found in the relevant chapter of Stahr et al's (2000) book.

Intense education and training
Once the initial self-assessment team was chosen they received the licensed assessor training.

Phased introduction of the Model concepts
Implementation commenced with a pilot self-assessment in a couple of areas, which was soon extended to a couple of other interested areas. A corporate assessment was undertaken during 1996 involving the senior management team. By 1996 individual divisions and departments were self-assessing using the Model.
Corporate usage of the Model criteria was phased, in that the main emphasis initially was leadership, processes and results.

Expert facilitation
The organisation trained its own staff to provide the expert facilitation.

Although on reflection they recommended a need for an external consultant (expert facilitator) to provide support in the early days. By 1999, two experienced external assessors were involved to support the award simulation approach that had more recently been adopted.

Good communications
Seen as vital during the implementation experience.

The use of quality tools
Quality tools were used prior to embarking upon the use of the EFQM Excellence Model, although the early self-assessments highlighted that the organisation's people knew very little about processes and about becoming a process centred organisation. Efforts to address this were put into place.

Securing quick successes
This was recognised as an area for improvement once the process had been initiated.

Celebrating success
By 1999, the organisation was seeking external recognition for celebrating its success evident by the submission for the Excellence North-East Award. External recognition and thereby celebration continued as in 1999 STAHT was recognised as one of the three National Specialist Learning Centres within the NHS. The Trust had learnt a great deal over the six years and increasingly received requests for visits or to provide presentations at national seminars and conferences. A culture of commitment, involvement and enthusiasm now prevails.

Recognising staff
The leadership steering group undertook a major review of staff recognition mechanisms within the Trust. The review highlighted some areas for improvement, which were subsequently addressed.

Having in place a process that ensures everyone is responsible for achieving excellence
By 1999, all areas of the Trust were actively involved in improvement activities which implied the organisational culture was one that reflected excellence.

Committing ongoing resources
Resources were committed for education and training opportunities and for the self-assessments, the latter utilising considerable staff time when an award

simulation approach was used during 1999. It was not clear what resources were allocated towards information systems, although what was clear was that the information was not readily available to the corporate assessment team during 1996.

*Apply RADAR logic to implementation strategy*
Assessment and review was undertaken early into the implementation programme and the learning captured. In essence the main lessons learned were that the Model terminology at the time was very alien to clinical staff, it was crucial to involve medical staff at the beginning of the programme and it was imperative that the action plans were kept to a manageable size.

The improvement actions resulting from the assessment and review included changing the Model language so that it was familiar to its users, including medical staff in the assessor training programme and prioritising improvement actions emerging from the self-assessments.

When the organisation applied the award simulation approach in 1999, they observed that the accuracy and validity of the self-assessment was compromised when time and commitment from people was decreased.

*Other factors observed*
Action oriented – The Trust observed that prior to using the Model improvement areas were identified and yet action was not taken to address these. An example being that patient and General Practitioner surveys had previously been carried out but very little action was taken as a result. More recently action was being taken to address the areas for improvement that had been identified.

Emerging advice – As a result of using the award simulation approach, STAHT were disappointed with the agreed score of 217 points. Particularly as they had perceived that they were a 'good' organisation. In view of this finding, the Trust advised users of the Model to be prepared to accept disappointment.

Change is sustainable – What was very evident from STAHT was that the approach taken had resulted in sustainable efforts towards healthcare excellence that had gone, and appeared to be going, from strength to strength.

## Wakefield and Pontefract Community Health NHS Trust
Details obtained from Stahr et al (2000).

*TQM Maturity*
The organisation had been applying quality concepts since 1993. The tools used were audit, continuous quality improvement agendas, developing a local

Patients' Charter and Investors in People. In 1995, the Quality, Evaluation and Development Department was formed to review quality models and frameworks.

*Set up a steering committee with appropriate representation*
A self-assessment team was set up that contained an Executive Director, represented a wide range of the areas within the Trust and had the full support of the Chief Executive.

*Develop a vision for excellence*
The vision for excellence was made clear in that using the EFQM Excellence Model would secure a culture of continuous improvement in addition to providing an overarching framework for the quality initiatives in existence. Clear objectives were determined.

*Develop a strategy for implementation*
An implementation strategy was developed which mirrored the one provided at the time by the EFQM because it was felt to meet the determined objectives. The strategy also contained detailed roles, responsibilities and timescales.

*Implement strategy*

Visible Chief Executive Commitment
The Chief Executive had demonstrated relentless commitment for using the EFQM Excellence Model, which was believed to have been invaluable.

Integration
Integration did not occur at first but it was suggested that the action plan emerging from the self-assessment should have been incorporated into the Directors' objectives and business plans as not doing so compromised improvement actions relating to the areas to address. More recently the EFQM Excellence Model was used to support the delivery of clinical governance. Five years into the journey full integration had been achieved.

Launch
A decision was made to keep the process low-key and so a '*big bang*' launch was purposefully avoided.

## Intense education and training
A self-assessment team was established in 1995 of which all the members received intense education and training in the use of the EFQM Excellence Model from an expert facilitator.

## Phased introduction of the Model concepts
The assessment team were expected to apply all the Model concepts.

## Expert facilitation
A British Quality Foundation accredited consultant provided expert facilitation.

## Good communications
Communications centred around informing the assessment team of the impact that self-assessment would have on their normal operational roles. Self-assessment plans were communicated to people who needed to be involved. Hence, communications were effected on a need to know basis.

## The use of quality tools
Quality tools had been used for improving processes.

## Securing quick successes
The self-assessment team learned how to make the self-assessment process more efficient by being more selective with the information collected. Secondly, the team tried to secure efficiencies by documenting strengths and areas for improvement in as few words as possible, only to find the statements often didn't make sense at a later date.

## Celebrating success
No evidence found in the text.

## Recognising staff
No evidence found in the text.

## Having in place a process that ensures everyone is responsible for achieving excellence
The EFQM Excellence Model has promoted involvement of the organisation's people in the pursuit of excellence.

## Committing ongoing resources
Time was protected to undergo the data collection and self-assessment exercise. A resource room was allocated for the data emerging from the self-

assessment. The time and energy required for undertaking a self-assessment was underestimated.

*Apply RADAR logic to implementation strategy*
A co-ordinator was nominated to ensure the action plan remained on track, which involved regular review meetings. A review of the overall self-assessment process was conducted prior to preparing for subsequent ones.

*Other factors observed*
Rigour - The self-assessment was the most thorough, searching and testing organisational diagnosis that had been carried out within the Trust.
Learning – The people within the organisation learned that there was no understanding or review of processes.
Terminology – Whilst there were occasions when the meaning behind some of the language needed to be interpreted, it by no means created any difficulties.
Scoring – In the initial phase there was insufficient expertise to score effectively or efficiently. As a result much time was wasted debating scores. In hindsight scoring should have been applied to the process at a later date, as it was not accurate initially, despite the time and effort applied to it.


**Burton Hospitals NHS Trust**
At the time of writing the Trust had only been actively using the Model for approximately ten months.

*TQM Maturity*
Audit, customer surveys and taking appropriate action had been a regular feature within the Hospital.

*Set up a steering committee with appropriate representation*
The membership of the steering committee was the Chief Executive, the Medical Director and the Lead for Clinical Governance and other quality initiatives.

*Develop a vision for excellence*
The vision for excellence mirrored the concepts of the Model.

*Develop a strategy for implementation*
The strategy developed for implementation contained the following steps.
1. Awareness sessions for senior managers and clinicians.
2. Individual departmental interviews with senior team members conducted by the expert facilitator in order to determine desired Customer, People,

Society and Key Performance Results.

3. Each departmental team were to encourage wider involvement in agreeing the results that would be subjected to self-assessment.

4. Self-assessment against results areas identified was to be undertaken, thereby not using the enabler section of the Model at that stage.

5. Each team were to undergo a Chief Executive Review to agree priorities for action (embark upon the enablers aspect of the Model), provide support and coaching and develop further understanding.

6. Each department was to effect improvement actions and review progress.

7. A best practice workshop was planned following the first round of Chief Executive Reviews designed to share the learning, celebrate early successes, inform the teams of the next steps and demonstrate the Chief Executive's commitment towards using the EFQM Excellence Model.

8. A cycle of six-monthly chief executive reviews and annual best practice workshops was to be put in place. Parallel activities were to be eliminated thereby integrating the Model into everyday practice.

9. At an appropriate time personnel within Burton Hospitals were to share the learning with the other NHS organisations.

*Implement strategy*

Visible Chief Executive Commitment

The Chief Executive commitment in Burton Hospitals was visible, extensive and admirable. For instance, the Chief Executive attended each review within the first cycle (at the time of writing only the first cycle had been completed). Furthermore, by becoming so involved in the process he soon grasped the fundamental principles of the Model and the difference between enablers and results. Armed with this knowledge, the Chief Executive was able to explain to the teams the purpose of using the Model, in addition to providing coaching in its application.

During the reviews the Chief Executive actively encouraged teams to prioritise their activities. By way of an example, one team expressed the difficulties associated with one outpatient initiative that was mainly due to the lack of time available for training. However, it seemed that the team preferred to deal with the day to day irritants of the failing system rather than use the time they spent overcoming these irritants, on training the relevant staff. The Chief Executive therefore asked the team why they could not undertake the necessary training by the end of the week. The team did not have an answer. They were happy with the idea, and so prioritised this aspect of service promising to complete the training before the end of the week. The reviews were set up and supported in such a way that the improvement actions subject to deadlines were followed up, in a timely manner by or on behalf of the Chief Executive.

Similar events occurred during the twenty-five plus reviews, which further motivated the organisation into action.  In some instances, the teams required assistance from the Chief Executive who was enthusiastic to help irrespective of the task at hand.  Examples of these tasks included identifying resources, supporting the development of the information system and personally becoming involved in interface issues.

<u>Integration</u>

The plan incorporated an element that would support integration.  Examples included integrating the monthly audit afternoon, clinical governance and controls assurance (risk management) into the self-assessment process and replacing the Directors' meetings with Chief Executive Reviews.

<u>Launch</u>

A workshop was planned for informing the senior management team of the Trust's intention to use the EFQM Excellence Model.

<u>Intense education and training</u>

Minimal education and training was planned.  Instead the implementation process was to concentrate on learning by doing thereby avoiding misalignment between theory and practice.

<u>Phased introduction of the Model concepts</u>

The implementation strategy supported a phased introduction of the Model concepts to the whole organisation.

<u>Expert facilitation</u>

The team working for a dedicated NHS Learning Centre provided the expert facilitation, and informed the implementation strategy.

<u>Good communications</u>

Communications were effectively managed on a timely, need to know basis.

<u>The use of quality tools</u>

At the time of writing the process had not reached sufficient maturity for using generic quality tools.

<u>Securing quick successes</u>

A number of quick successes were realised in impressive time frames.  For instance, a number of departments secured significant successes within two months of using the Model.

Celebrating success

Success was celebrated at the best practice workshop. The Chairman also acknowledged the successes of the Trust during a presentation at a national healthcare conference, which contained healthcare personnel from a number of European countries.

Recognising staff

The efforts of staff towards continuous improvement were recognised by the Chief Executive. In some instances this took the form of personal correspondence and in others public verbal recognition during workshops and other events.

Having in place a process that ensures everyone is responsible for achieving excellence

The Chief Executive Review promoted active involvement of all staff within the Trust. So much so that in one instance the secretary took the lead in presenting the outcome of the team's self-assessment. Furthermore, it was not uncommon for staff nurses, physiotherapists, ward sisters, secretaries and clerks to attend the Chief Executive reviews with their senior management team. Conducting the reviews in this manner further supported the Chief Executive to visibly demonstrate his commitment and common sense approach towards excellence.

Committing ongoing resources

Resources were committed for the expert facilitation and the time spent to implement the process and to further develop the information systems.

*Apply RADAR logic to implementation strategy*

The RADAR logic was not applied to the implementation strategy.

*Other factors observed*

Prioritising tangible improvements – What was noticeable in Burton Hospitals was the focus on continuous improvement as oppose to the specifics of the Model, an approach, that facilitated the achievement of quick successes.

Results focus – Many teams experienced difficulties with differentiating between enablers and results. Indeed this was the biggest challenge and cause of anxiety. Particularly as some senior managers (including Directors) were threatened by their lack of understanding in relation to enablers and results, a situation that was to be handled by the continuous drive for using the Model and the passage of time for facilitating further understanding.

## Lockside Medical Centre (A small general practice)

*TQM Maturity*

The practice had not really used recognised generic quality tools before EFQM although there was a real customer focus amongst the whole team. A sound clinical audit system was in operation prior to embarking upon the EFQM Excellence Model.

*Set up a steering committee with appropriate representation*

The total number of employees within the practice amounted to seventeen and so a formal steering committee was not set up, although all three general practitioners and the practice manager took an active role in leading the process.

*Develop a vision for excellence*

Lockside Medical Centre knew that it wanted to be a very good practice from the patient's, employees, wider society, Health Authority and governing body's perspective. The people within the practice also wanted to apply sound, well-respected clinical and managerial methodologies.

*Develop a strategy for implementation*

The strategy developed contained similar elements to that of Burton Hospitals as the same team provided expert facilitation for both organisations.

1. An awareness session was held for senior practice staff.

2. Individual interviews were conducted by the expert facilitator with each member of the team including secretaries, clerks, nurses, domestics and general practitioners in order to determine desired Customer, People, Society and Key Performance Results from each team member's perspective.

3. A feedback workshop was held to share all the results areas identified.

4. The overall team agreed the results that would be subjected to self-assessment.

5. The team undertook a self-assessment against the results areas identified, thereby not using the enabler section of the Model.

6. Improvement actions and a review for progress were undertaken.

7. The original plan was to progress towards applying self-assessment to the enabler criteria.

8. The original plan was to put in place a cycle of yearly reviews by the whole team.

9. The team was to share their learning with other general practices and the wider NHS.

The overall theme was to use the concepts of the Model in preference to applying the specifics.

*Implement strategy*

## Visible Chief Executive Commitment

All the general practitioners and the practice manager demonstrated visible commitment for striving for Excellence. They all took personal action to secure improvements.

## Integration

The main integration challenge was collecting information practically and on a daily basis to assess overall performance.

## Launch

An initial practice meeting was held to share with the team the process that was to be supported by the facilitator. In hindsight this was pitched too much on the Model structure at the expense of the concepts.

## Intense education and training

Intense education and training was avoided, the intention being that efforts would be focused on making things better rather than understanding a comprehensive management model.

## Phased introduction of the Model concepts

The Model concepts were introduced in a phased manner. So much so that at the time of writing the practice was intending not to apply self-assessment to the enabler criteria of the Model. Preferring to concentrate on demonstrating positive trends in relation to the results areas identified.

## Expert facilitation

Provided.

## Good communications

Timely communications were handled on a need to know basis.

## The use of quality tools

Generic quality tools were not used by the practice.

## Securing quick successes

Successes were secured so quickly that the corrective actions were undertaken during the time the facilitator had suggested should be used for data gathering. To explain, the practice was advised to collect data around a number of irritants within the system. Examples included things like medical records not being available for surgery, prescriptions not being ready on time and unnecessarily chasing up of ambulance requests. The plan was to quickly apply Pareto analysis to the data so that priorities for action could be identified. However, when the facilitator visited Lockside Medical Centre to undertake the Pareto analysis, the practice team had already identified their priority areas and put corrective actions in place, all in less than two weeks.

## Celebrating success

Despite only having used the Model for approximately six months the first opportunity to celebrate success came when the practice was asked to contribute to a national conference. The presentation was well received, thought provoking and demonstrated leading edge thinking within the practice. The team were already adept at celebrating their successes so this aspect was a significant characteristic of the implementation process.

## Recognising staff

Recognising the achievements and valuing the efforts of staff was a normal feature of the organisation prior to using the EFQM Excellence Model and so nothing changed in this respect. In saying that though the practice did develop a people perception questionnaire with the facilitator, based on the findings from the individual interviews and a questionnaire used by another healthcare organisation. Consequently, the tool was very relevant to the specific issues within the practice in addition to being externally focused enough to support benchmarking.

## Having in place a process that ensures everyone is responsible for achieving excellence

Everyone was keen to be involved in the process, although again this was not a significant difference in the practice and previous to applying the Model all the members of the team were enthusiastic about providing a good service.

## Committing ongoing resources

Resources in terms of time for the data gathering, self-assessments, corrective actions and reviews were readily committed. Given the small size of the team, the time taken to use the results aspect of the Model was in fact significant. Information systems were also aligned to the pursuit of excellence.

### *Apply RADAR logic to implementation strategy*

The RADAR logic was not applied to the implementation strategy.

*Other factors observed*

Action oriented team – All the members of Lockside Medical Centre were happy to take action towards continuous improvement. They appreciated that nothing would change unless they made it happen. The team also applied a common sense approach to improvements, which made taking action easier.

In the right hands – The way the practice only applied a small element of the Model and yet still managed to secure significant improvements indicated that it did not matter which quality tool was used when the organisation was so keen to improve. Hence, in the right hands any quality tool will make a difference, because in reality it is the people that make the difference, not the Model.

Measuring what it important – A particularly innovative outcome to emerge from Lockside Medical Centre was that the general practitioners undertook a literature review to determine which treatment interventions were the most effective. In total seven treatment interventions were associated with saving the most lives. Furthermore, 25% more lives could have been saved if the practice adopted these treatment interventions, which meant that out of the typical 120 deaths per year, at least 30 of these could be avoided. This approach was adopted.

Networking – An emergent theme from this example and the others previously analysed is that the key people from all the healthcare organisations made considerable efforts to ensure that they became part of the networks that related to using the EFQM Excellence Model within healthcare. As a consequence they became exposed to and were able to share good and/or best practices, were regularly in the company of like-minded people and made considerable efforts to compliment their internal perspectives with external ones.

Lose focus – A concern that the facilitator had in relation to not using the Model concepts was that the practice could lose focus or apply efforts to areas that were not important in the ever changing world of healthcare.

## Unsuccessful Implementation approaches within healthcare

*A district general hospital providing acute and community services*
Details obtained from published literature and personal knowledge of the organisation.

*TQM Maturity*
Early in 1993 the organisation began using the Malcolm Baldridge National Quality Award (MBNQA) framework within some departments before transferring to the EFQM Excellence Model in 1996.

*Set up a steering committee with appropriate representation*
A distinct steering committee was not set up, rather a quality manager was appointed.

*Develop a vision for excellence*
Whilst there was a drive for using self-assessment and taking improvement action, a vision clarifying the characteristics of excellence was not developed.

*Develop a strategy for implementation*
A strategy was developed for using self-assessment although ownership was limited and where it was owned; involvement in its delivery sporadic.


*Implement strategy*
Visible Chief Executive Commitment
When the organisation embarked upon using self-assessment there was total Chief Executive commitment. However, in 1997 the Chief Executive moved on and was replaced by someone who had limited understanding of the EFQM Excellence Model. Furthermore, the new Chief Executive perceived the Model as a 'tick-box' exercise that delivered no tangible benefits for the organisation at all. Consequently Chief Executive commitment for using the Model was lacking.


Integration
Different departments within the organisation could choose whether or not they adopted the Model and so integration into everyday working practices was not achieved or strived for. The departments that chose to use the Model were mixed in terms of their clinical and non-clinical remits.


Launch
A specific launch was not part of the implementation strategy.

Intense education and training
The quality manager received intense education and training and was expected to disseminate the learning within the organisation. Networking opportunities were exploited by the quality manager, which widened the input into the training and development opportunities provided by the Trust. In 1999 the quality manager was made redundant and so intense training for the remaining members of the organisation, in relation to the EFQM Excellence Model ceased.

## Phased introduction of the Model concepts

In view of departments being given the opportunity to choose whether they used the Model or not, the implementation process could be viewed as being phased. However, the approach taken by the departments applying the Model was the workshop approach, which meant the teams were exposed to all the Model concepts at once, a situation, that caused anxiety for some members of the teams.

## Expert facilitation

Some departments received expert facilitation by external management consultants. Noticeably the department that received support from IBM in the initial phases emerged as the most successful users and achievers of the EFQM Excellence Model. In time the quality manager became an expert facilitator, although this skill was not valued by the organisation as much as it was valued by contacts outside the organisation thereby having a detrimental effect on the internal input from this particular facilitator.

## Good communications

Communications within the teams using self-assessment was good although there was no overall communication strategy for the use of the Model.

## The use of quality tools

Teams within the organisation did not readily use generic quality tools.

## Securing quick successes

The learning that emerged from the departments using the EFQM Excellence Model recognised the importance of securing quick successes even though they did not realise this initially. What was noticeable from one department was that improvement actions were prioritised in relation to the immediate needs of department and so efforts to address the areas for improvement received much support, an approach that was recommended. A further observation was that the department (a clinical one) embarked upon inward looking, safe projects initially before they tackled outward looking, more complex projects. Examples of the outward looking projects included benchmarking, undertaking customer driven quality audits and successfully applying for Investors in People and Charter Mark Awards.

## Celebrating success

The organisation readily and frequently supported the departments using the Model and celebrated successes in a timely manner.

Recognising staff
Staff securing healthcare improvements were recognised informally and formally.

Having in place a process that ensures everyone is responsible for achieving excellence
Not everyone was expected to achieve excellence and so not everyone worked towards it.

Committing ongoing resources
Resources were not singled out for using the EFQM Excellence Model other than those relating to the appointment of the quality manager and the provision of internal training and development.

*Apply RADAR logic to implementation strategy*
The RADAR logic was not applied to the implementation strategy.

*Other factors observed*
The right tool needs to be in the right hands – The organisation contained many people who criticised the Model for being something that did not deliver tangible benefits. However, what was observed was that where there was commitment and action; using the EFQM Excellence Model was beneficial in terms of improving the quality of healthcare. Thereby suggesting that the appropriateness of the tool to do the job (in this case the EFQM Excellence Model) is irrelevant if the tool is in the wrong hands. An analogy can be made here with an electric drill in that it would be irrelevant how excellent that drill was for doing its job, the author would still not be able to drill a neat hole!
Benefits attained – In the areas using the Model, benefits attained included good staff development and cross functional working, improvements in recruiting staff and undertaking individual performance review, an acceptance that continuous improvement was positive and that *incremental* change was preferable as well as sustainable.
Scoring – One directorate in particular used the scoring profile of the Model and was able to demonstrate year on year improvements that motivated people and supported the process for celebrating success.

*A rural maternity unit*
Details obtained from personal experience.

*TQM Maturity*
Audit and customer surveys had been used in the maternity unit prior to

embarking upon the use of the EFQM Excellence Model. However, there was a lack of tangible improvement action resulting from both these methods.

*Set up a steering committee with appropriate representation*
A steering committee was set up consisting of the Head of Midwifery and senior managers within the department. In total there were eight members, although the commitment for the process was not the same for each of these members, ranging from active resistance to obsessional commitment.

*Develop a vision for excellence*
Clarity was provided to the senior team regarding a definition of excellence.

*Develop a strategy for implementation*
An implementation strategy was agreed by the steering committee that was influenced by the advice of Øvretveit (1999) who recommended that team should be prepared to amend the original plan so that commitment from all the team was paramount to the timing of the implementation steps. The strategy involved the following steps:- a one day workshop for self-assessing against the enablers within the Model, a series of meetings to determine the results from the enablers identified, a data gathering process in relation to the results identified (not the enablers at this stage), an accurate self-assessment relating to the unit's results (to indicate actual performance in relation to Customers, People, Society and Key Performance Results), prioritisation of improvement actions, taking action to secure improvements, reviewing progress and moving on to use the whole of the EFQM Excellence Model. Scoring was not a feature of the implementation approach.

*Implement strategy*
Visible Chief Executive Commitment
There was no visible Chief Executive commitment. The best that was achieved was an agreement that the 'project' could go ahead with a view that the Chief Executive would only be interested if benefits were realised.

Integration
Minimal integration was achieved as the implementation process only lasted seven months.

Launch
It was determined that there would be no public launch within the unit, rather the journey commenced with a one day workshop held at a venue external to the hospital.

Intense education and training
A number of presentations were provided prior to the one-day self-assessment workshop. In addition, one-to-one support to understand and apply the concepts was provided by the expert facilitator. Visits to other units and other networking and learning opportunities were identified and exploited.

Phased introduction of the Model concepts
The Model concepts were phased in that the approach involved undertaking a self-assessment against the enablers initially and then identifying the results that these enablers were to influence. Once the result areas had been identified the data collection process to determine actual performance was commenced. It was soon after this stage that the Head of Midwifery who was also the expert facilitator left the organisation.

Expert facilitation
The Head of Midwifery provided expert facilitation at the outset.

Good communications
Communications with the steering committee were effective.

The use of quality tools
The implementation process did not reach the stage where generic quality tools would have been beneficial.

Securing quick successes
Some quick successes were achieved, one being the setting up of a customer perception working group involving a number of enthusiastic midwives. The group applied credible research findings and consulted the unit staff widely to prepare a generic customer perception questionnaire. Previous to the generic questionnaire several versions had been used by as many differing distribution means. Secondly a working group was initiated to consider how best the unit could identify and respond to the perceptions of the unit's people. There was a real feel of excitement for this new way of working amongst the front-line staff who had felt suppressed for quite some time.

Also, the senior management team began to recognise that they had been working without a clear vision, targets or a sound performance measurement system.

Even within the seven months insights began to change and behaviours followed. For instance, managers recognised that in the main they devised and executed plans but never identified a review and improvement process. The rotation protocol for midwives was one such example. Secondly, target setting and performance measurement was not a feature associated with the day to day running of the unit until the principles of the EFQM Excellence Model were adopted.

Celebrating success
Implementation did not reach the stage where it was appropriate to celebrate successes.

Recognising staff
Staff were recognised informally by the Head of Midwifery, although this required a significant change in culture before it could be seen as the norm from everyone.
Having in place a process that ensures everyone is responsible for achieving excellence
Each member of the senior team within the unit was expected to be involved in the process. Even so, no one was expected to take on more than they could accommodate from a time and a conceptual understanding perspective.

Committing ongoing resources
Resources were committed for the one-day self-assessment workshop and time was prioritised to undertake the work required for ingraining the EFQM Excellence Model into everyday practice.

*Apply RADAR logic to implementation strategy*
The RADAR logic was not applied to the implementation strategy.

*Other factors observed*
Managing improvement projects – The team recognised that the improvement projects within the department needed co-ordinating to avoid duplication and support the sharing of learning. Hence, a senior team member agreed to undertake the task of co-ordinating improvement projects. Good project management as advised by Øvretveit (1999) was also applied, in that project teams were set up with clear aims, reporting agreements, measurement arrangements and facilitation.
Terminology – The team did not experience much difficulty applying the Model terminology to midwifery.
Overfacing – There was a risk of being overfaced by the findings of the self-assessment. To explain 68 areas for improvement were identified in the enabler criteria alone which in turn impacted on 205 different result areas, and that was just for a maternity unit. The information needs of the unit were also challenged suggesting that involvement of the information department is best secured at the start of the journey rather than somewhere in the middle.

<u>Views of managers</u> – At times the process was uncomfortable for managers who did not readily learn from others or who were happier when they felt everything was going well as opposed to realising there was no evidence to confirm this and in some instances everything was not going well. It would be helpful if managers were realistically informed of the 'pain' and the 'pleasure' associated with using the EFQM Excellence Model at the outset of the journey. On the other hand, the team did begin to appreciate the need for evidence to confirm their assumptions and were supportive of this rigorous approach.

<u>Training</u> – During the training sessions there was repeated requests for healthcare examples relating to the use of the EFQM Excellence Model, therefore the expert facilitator needed to have plenty of these to hand.

## Characteristics associated with successful implementation within healthcare

The characteristics associated with successful implementation of the EFQM Excellence Model within healthcare have been determined from analysing the approaches described and by supplementing that analysis with further knowledge gained from the substantial experience of working within this field. The 'Implementation Framework' has been used to present the characteristics in a format that is now familiar to the reader.

**Summary Box: Characteristics of successful implementation.**

- TQM Maturity
- Steering Committee
- Vision for Excellence
- Strategy for implementation
- Chief Executive committment
- Integration
- Launch
- Intensive education and training
- Phased introduction of concepts
- Expert facilitation
- Good communications
- Use of quality tools
- Securing quick successes
- Celebrating success
- Recognising staff
- Involving everyone
- Resources
- Applying RADAR logic

*TQM Maturity*

Irrespective of what quality tools and concepts have been previously used, it is the organisational cultural characteristics that influence successful implementation of the EFQM Excellence Model into healthcare practice. For instance if there already is a 'can-do' attitude, a customer focus and a culture of valuing staff then the challenge is less demanding.

A familiarity with audit, performance measurement and securing tangible improvements into service delivery will enable the process. However, the skills required of audit, measurement and improvement can be taught fairly quickly whereas changing behaviours and organisational norms take longer. Hence any lack of skill in relation to using quality tools and excellence frameworks is not a major issue with regards to the likelihood of successful implementation. It is worth remembering that it is not the excellence of the tool that will secure successful implementation, rather it is the 'hands' that that tool is in that will make the difference.

If some of the organisation cultural characteristics highlighted in the initial paragraph of this section are not a feature of the organisation then it may be advisable to develop core values and behaviours and gain some success in achieving those before embarking upon using the EFQM Excellence Model within healthcare.

*Set up a steering committee with appropriate representation*

A steering group is recommended for at least agreeing the vision of excellence and the desired characteristics of that vision, determining the implementation strategy and its discrete steps, and ensuring RADAR logic is applied to the chosen implementation strategy. Other roles and responsibilities of the group would be determined on an organisationally specific basis. However, what is imperative is that it contains a team of senior personnel (clinical and non-clinical) who are committed to the fundamental principles of excellence and willing to act as role models for the organisation.

It is preferable that the Chief Executive is a member of the steering committee or at least that s/he personally influences the membership and visibly supports its activities. The size of the steering group would obviously reflect the size and resources available to the organisation. This in mind, the steering group may decide to set up a self-assessment team or a number of self-assessment teams to support the implementation process.

*Develop a vision for excellence*

A clear vision and the characteristics of that vision need to be determined at the outset. Similarly, specific performance measures need to be agreed in order that the application of RADAR logic can take place. It is advisable to have a realistic vision and therefore not consider scoring or applying for an award in the initial phase. The vision could contain the fundamental principles of the Model, a 'can-do' attitude and the aim that the EFQM Excellence Model will be the overarching framework for all the initiatives, imperatives and quality approaches used by the organisation. Although what is more important is that the vision is owned by the steering committee.

Once the vision is agreed specific objectives will need to be determined to support the operational aspects of implementation.

## Develop a strategy for implementation

Develop a strategy to achieve the vision for excellence. Whilst it is recognised that the strategy will need to address the unique needs of the organisation, it may not be necessary to totally reinvent the wheel. Learning from others in healthcare is recommended here. Once the strategy is agreed it will be useful to clarify the roles and responsibilities of the steering committee and other personnel key to the implementation process. Further advice would include being prepared to amend the strategy dependent upon the learning attained from applying the RADAR logic.

## Implement strategy

### Visible Chief Executive Commitment

Chief Executive commitment is imperative, otherwise applying the EFQM Excellence Model into the organisation will fail. Furthermore, that Chief Executive commitment needs to be relentless and visible. What this means in practice is that if a Chief Executive review process is part of the implementation strategy then the Chief Executive should attend each review. In addition, if teams are expected to submit their self-assessments to the Chief Executive by a certain deadline, for instance 10-14 days before the review, then the Chief Executive needs to ensure that s/he is seen as having allocated sufficient time to read them before the review takes place. Experience has shown that teams put significant effort into preparing the self-assessment documentation for the reviews and therefore expect the Chief Executive to match that effort with sufficient time to digest its contents. Hence a recommendation not to hold a review on the first day that the Chief Executive returns from annual leave.

An all-inclusive approach to the reviews will enable the Chief Executive to demonstrate enthusiasm and commitment towards continuous improvement to both junior and senior members of the organisation. And given the extensive demands on Chief Executives, the inclusive approach may also prove to be good use of his or her time.

Secondly, the Chief Executive should become personally involved in improvement projects and if in place attend as many of the organisation's Quality Award ceremonies as possible. S/he should constantly strive for *all* the senior members of the organisation (Directors, senior clinicians and managers) to be signed up to the process. A weak link in the senior management level of the organisation is problematic and detrimental to the process.

Integration
Integrating the EFQM Excellence Model into everyday practice is imperative for long-term success. Nevertheless integration efforts do not need to be applied at the outset rather they can be explored and developed throughout the process. A recommended activity that will secure integration in the long-term is the regular cycle of Chief Executive Reviews. Once this process has been set up, efforts can begin to include clinical governance, controls assurance and other such frameworks (current or future) into the departmental and organisational self-assessments, thereby eradicating the feeling that using the EFQM Excellence Model is an add-on. Organisations experienced in using the Model align their business planning and departmental operational planning processes into the self-assessment cycle. The expert facilitator can support this process.

Launch
Holding a launch was not seen as a vital element for success. However, the steering committee do need to consider whether a launch would be beneficial and if they decide it will be whether the launch should be low key or 'big bang'. It is important though that the drive for using the Model is constant, and helping this may include regular promotional activities to boost the organisation's efforts towards excellence.

Complacency has no place in using the EFQM Excellence Model for securing improvements in healthcare.

Intense education and training
Education and training needs depend upon the vision, implementation approach and existing skills within the organisation. Consequently, it is important to ensure that the education and training approach agreed takes into account all of these factors. It is also advisable to consider the resource implication and likelihood of achieving an enthusiastic training and development strategy.

Do not underestimate learning by doing and the support available from the expert facilitator, particularly when it comes to understanding the difference between enablers and results. Include networking opportunities, visiting other units and sharing best practice within the organisation. In line with this thinking is the option of by-passing too much education and training in relation to the theoretical concepts and structure of the Model, an approach that would avoid over theorising in preference for keeping it practical and within the workplace.

In view of Salford's experience, the steering committee may need to consider wider education and training programmes related to change management, communication, action planning and managing a project improvement team.

### Phased introduction of the Model concepts

Phasing the introduction of the Model concepts is a preferable approach for healthcare. Whether it be starting with results to enablers, or enablers to results is probably less important providing the linkages are explicit and the understanding that *how we do things* directly influences *what we achieve* is secured. Applying a full self-assessment often means users focus on the specifics of the Model rather than it's concepts and so ought to be avoided. A further recommendation would be to apply the scoring matrix once there is a history of successful improvements in the organisation and a good understanding of the Model concepts, its specific sub-criteria and how both relate to healthcare.

Starting the process by way of pilot sites is not recommended as it gives a diluted message of commitment and means that not everyone need be involved in striving for excellence, an approach which could invoke ethical concerns.

### Expert facilitation

Expert facilitation, preferably external to the organisation is a must. Furthermore the expert facilitator must have a repertoire of success stories in healthcare, an experience of applying the model and its terminology into a healthcare environment and must be used to dealing with the regular queries emerging from healthcare personnel.

The expert facilitator must therefore be able to provide support for understanding the difference between healthcare enablers and healthcare results. S/he must also be aware and able to deal with the fact that clinicians are more comfortable with cause and effect relationships rather than associations, and that, associations are acceptable in the pursuit of continuous improvement. This poses a challenge in relation to gaining support from clinical members of the team.

### Good communications

Best results were seen when the communications strategy was based on a when to know and need to know rationale. Obviously, the approach would be determined by the steering committee. If communications are provided on a when to know, need to know basis then it could be helpful to set up an intranet site containing details of the process and its progress. Should this be done it would provide a communications contingency and be an avenue for members of the organisation who are outside the need to know category but express an interest in the process.

Aspects that were seen as valuable to the process were communicating messages that confirmed areas for improvement were not going to be associated with blame, people would be given time to learn and that the process was not another initiative, rather it was here to stay.

A further recommendation focuses on managing the expectations of the organisation's people. Therefore users of the Model need to know that it is a demanding approach that can be demoralising and disappointing at times. Especially when personnel have felt they were doing a good job or had undertaken improvement activities that they thought would benefit, only to find that the self-assessment showed otherwise. Similarly, the self-assessment can illuminate an overwhelming number of areas for improvement that need addressing which in turn can have a demotivating effect unless it is expected.

Despite the recommendation of securing quick successes, using the EFQM Excellence Model will not provide a 'quick fix' solution for any of the organisation's problems. As a result this message needs to be communicated along with a clear understanding of what continuous improvement means. An explanation of the latter is given by referring to a real life example. A team looking at integrated care pathways uncovered that in one Accident and Emergency care pathway, a patient's history was taken eight times. When asked what their goal would be in relation to continuous improvement the reply was achieving a care process that only involved one history taking. Whilst this intention was commendable it was also probably unrealistic in one continuous improvement activity. Therefore the team were advised to aim for seven history takings in the first instance, six in the next and so on, an approach that better reflects *incremental* continuous improvement. Using the EFQM Excellence Model should be challenging not fatal. The recommendation to keep it simple and achievable in the interests of securing long-term commitment towards excellence, is always helpful.

Experience has demonstrated that the above type of thinking creates difficulties for healthcare personnel as they want to strive for excellence when they see a gap in the system and yet the organisation in which they work makes it very difficult and in some instances seemingly impossible. Do not underestimate the resistance associated with promoting an *incremental* approach towards excellence.

Explain that understanding the Model can sometimes feel painful as it challenges people's thinking in relation to what healthcare results are. Hence understanding the difference between enablers and results can be difficult and so a message needs to be communicated that the organisation will support time to learn.

## The use of quality tools
A certain level of maturity in terms of total quality management is required before generic quality tools can be successfully applied. Healthcare personnel do not readily align to the quality tools that have emerged from industry and so ought not to be pushed to use them. Furthermore, a common sense approach to problem solving or undertaking improvements is a useful start and so should not be dismissed.

Nevertheless, generic quality tools do have a place in healthcare and so could be used when the common sense approach has not achieved the desired results or when the team are struggling to identify a suitable strategy for the area to address. This way the team will welcome using the quality tool rather than resist it.

## Securing quick successes
Securing quick successes is an important element in the journey towards excellence. Similar to this advice would be keeping action plans to a manageable size. Another recommendation worthy of consideration is to tackle areas that have been problematic for some time and work towards achieving quick successes with them first.

Remember to promote *incremental* continuous improvement to areas that align to the values of the team (providing these values mirror those of excellence); rather than tackle complex issues in their entirety at the outset which reflect the values of others outside the team, unless the issues are 'must dos'.

## Celebrating success
Regularly celebrate success internally and externally to the organisation and keep a register of them. An organisation quality award system is a useful approach for celebrating successes and for involving senior managers in the process, of which the latter is an enhancing ingredient.

## Recognising staff
Develop and promote a culture whereby staff are regularly recognised for their improvement efforts. Not everyone will work towards excellence and so it is important to recognise and value the staff who do. A factor to note here is that in many instances, recognition is more positively received from the Chief

Executive or direct line manager seen to be driving the EFQM Excellence Model implementation process, than anyone else in the organisation.

Recognising staff should include a sensitive approach to senior managers who feel threatened by the process, although they may still need their thinking and management style challenged on occasion.

### Having in place a process that ensures everyone is responsible for achieving excellence

Everyone should be expected to contribute towards the excellence journey thereby implying a pilot phase approach to implementation is not desirable. Communicating a message less demanding than everyone being expected to get involved will be detrimental in the long-term, especially if there is a change of C.E.O. In support of achieving total employee involvement, the Chief Executive and senior personnel (clinical and non-clinical) need to act as role models and all job descriptions should contain details of the responsibilities of the post holder in relation to the corporate pursuit of excellence.

An inclusive approach to the Chief Executive review will further strengthen the message that everyone has to be involved in the process which includes medical staff who often feel left out in such corporate endeavours. The advice from Salford to involve consultants early in the process is invaluable. Lastly, self-assessment should be applied to determine progress towards total involvement of the organisation's people.

### Committing ongoing resources

Second in importance to the organisation's people is accurate, timely and easily accessible information. However, having good information systems in place will probably be the most significant challenge as healthcare personnel often perceive this to be the most ineffective area of the service. The steering committee therefore needs to determine the potential resources required for aligning information systems to the needs of all the departments within the organisation, which may be significant given that information systems have been poorly related to clinicians' needs, (Stahr et al 2000). Furthermore, it should be noted that poor information systems would compromise the journey towards excellence and have an adverse effect on motivation.

In terms of other resources, it is recommended that a person, with the relevant skills and working at an appropriate level within the organisation be appointed to the post of facilitator. The role of the facilitator would be to support the Chief Executive review process, follow up action plans from the reviews and maybe co-ordinate a corporate self-assessment team for scoring the organisation. However, should the organisation consider applying for an award once a positive trend is seen in the overall scores, then the resource implications in terms of time should also be accommodated for.

Resources are obviously required for education and training. Although, in some instances securing these may only involve prioritising education and training opportunities. Experience has shown that healthcare wastes valuable resources on inappropriate education and training. A real life example demonstrating this comes from a maternity unit that funded midwives to attend one-day workshops on alternative pain relieving therapies when the organisation had a policy in place whereby alternative therapies could <u>not</u> be provided by any member of staff employed by the organisation. Secondly, the author recalls a conversation some years previously when a Director of Nursing expressed that over half a million pounds had been spent on education and training within her department and yet no tangible benefits could be seen for such an extensive resource.

Lastly, ongoing commitment and energy is a valuable resource for successful implementation and so the steering committee and the facilitator should be provided with resources for networking and spending time with like minded people in the wider healthcare field.

*Apply RADAR logic to implementation strategy*

Applying the RADAR logic to the implementation strategy is a must if progress is to be monitored and the message of continuous improvement reaffirmed. Applying the RADAR logic to the implementation strategy could lie within the remit of the internal facilitator, if one is appointed.

Secondly it is imperative that a process is in place to capture the lessons learned. One of the most valuable aspects of the Model is the learning that emerges from regular continuous improvement efforts and subsequent assessment and review. A feature, which supports the learning culture currently being strengthened within the NHS.

Thirdly, if the RADAR logic were not applied then the steering committee would be unable to determine which enablers were most significant in achieving the most success in terms of implementing the strategy, a vital ingredient for successful implementation and effective use of resources. There is no point applying implementation efforts that are ineffective.

*Further recommendations for success*

- Be prepared for a challenge and a lengthy journey.
- Do not stifle enthusiasm
- Do not stifle creativity. Implementing the EFQM Excellence Model within healthcare requires creativity and therefore risk taking, both difficult concepts to apply in a risk- adverse environment.
- Access the learning from other organisations and share your learning widely for the benefit of healthcare.

- Measure what is important but be prepared to make some mistakes and waste time in this area in the initial phase.
- Remember to believe and communicate the message that the EFQM Excellence Model is about 'making a difference' and if that is not happening a review of the process is needed because the Model is not being used correctly.

### Applying the Model in relation to organisational structure

Besides determining the appropriate implementation approach for the organisation, it may be helpful for leaders to consider whether they want *everyone* in the organisation to use the *whole* of the EFQM Excellence Model. For instance, is it practical that a ward sister, physiotherapist, laboratory technician, secretary and/or porter self-assess against all the 32 subcriteria of the Model?

Some would argue that it is not, which is why the following 'Levels of Use' have been identified. (See Figure 4.1) The 'Levels of Use' have not emerged from research findings rather they have been created by the author based on the experience and insights gained through supporting, working alongside and networking with healthcare organisations throughout Europe. It is therefore posed as a suggestion for realistically achieving an organisation's aims in which everyone is using and happy about using the EFQM Excellence Model in their day to day practice. The rationale behind creating the differing 'Levels of Use' is to organisationally apply the Model in such a way that it is sensitive to the workload, responsibilities and resource allocations of all healthcare staff.

### *Level One*

Apply the RADAR concept of the EFQM Excellence Model only. This level is recommended for front line staff with no direct-line managerial responsibility, for example a porter, secretary, nurse or doctor. The idea being that if a particular staff member is interested in securing continuous improvement in a certain area of their practice, they could do it within the rigour of the RADAR concept.

This would mean that the leader (porter, secretary, nurse, doctor) of the improvement project would need to:

- be clear about the Results they wanted to achieve,
- have identified a planned Approach with a clear rationale,
- have a system in place for appropriately Deploying that approach, and
- ensure that they have identified how they will undertake regular Assessment and Review of their approach, including the impact on the desired results.

This person could then feed those results up to their direct line manager, who would probably be working at Level Two or Three.

### Level Two

Apply the RADAR concept to own improvement project. Additionally, influence and encourage other improvement project leaders to undertake projects that ensures the department as a whole is addressing the Customer, People, Society and Key Performance Results criteria of the EFQM Excellence Model. Level Two is recommended for staff with direct-line managerial responsibility for one or two clinical or non-clinical areas, for example a ward sister, portering manager, or clinical lead.

The manager would therefore be required to meet the demands of the results element of the Model in addition to having a clear understanding of the key enablers impacting on these results areas. By way of reminder the definition for excellence in results means that the department would need to demonstrate positive trends and/or sustained good performance, meet appropriate targets, compare well with other organisations, make it explicit that the results were caused by the enablers (actions), and demonstrate that the scope of the results addressed the relevant departmental areas. (EFQM 1999a)

Accordingly, the manager would need to balance the needs of all the healthcare stakeholders (customers, people, society, governments and other interested personnel). It could also be assumed therefore, that a manager able to meet the rigour required for the four results criteria must have a good insight into the priorities of the department and so undertaking a self-assessment against all the 24 enablers is not a sensible use of the department's resources. Furthermore, given that the departmental resources are finite self-assessing against all the 24 enabler sub-criteria could detract the team from concentrating on its priorities thereby compromising overall performance.

The information available from concentrating on the results and key enablers could be forwarded to the next direct line manager, who in turn would incorporate this data into a wider self-assessment. Level Two could also be used for managers of two areas as a precursor to using Level Three.

### Level Three

Apply the RADAR concept to own improvement project area, influence and encourage other improvement project leaders to undertake projects that ensures the department is addressing all the four RESULTS criteria and the PEOPLE and PROCESSES enablers of the EFQM Excellence Model. The people enablers for Level Three would relate to the Leadership, People and possibly the Partnership element of Partnerships and Resources sub-criteria of the EFQM Excellence Model.

This level is recommended for staff with direct-line managerial responsibility for one area (if they have gained significant experience in using the Model at Level Two), or for two clinical or non-clinical areas.

Applying Level Three would involve the manager undertaking a self-assessment and demonstrating continuous improvement in seven, or slightly above if incorporating partnerships subcriteria of the nine criteria of the EFQM Excellence Model. Therefore the manager would not be expected to fully self-assess against the enablers: Policy and Strategy, and Partnerships and Resources. This would be left for people applying all the aspects of the EFQM Excellence Model (level four). This does not mean that they will not be applying managerial duties in the areas of Policy and Strategy and Partnerships and Resources; rather they would not be undertaking a self-assessment in relation to the 'ADAR' aspect of the RADAR logic.

The information available from concentrating on the seven (plus) criteria of the Model could be forwarded onto the next direct line manager, who in turn would incorporate this data into a wider self-assessment.

### Level Four
Apply the whole of the EFQM Excellence Model. This level is recommended for managers who are responsible for a specialty, or for 3 or more departments, for example Clinical Directors, Service Managers, General Managers and Executive Directors. The outcome of a self-assessment at this managerial level of the organisation would be submitted for support, discussion and recognition at the regular Chief Executive Reviews.

### Further considerations
Obviously a variation of the above 'Levels of Use' could be determined by the particular organisation embarking upon the journey of using the EFQM Excellence Model. What would need to be taken into consideration though is how the different levels integrate with each other and what the overall approach would look like. For a diagrammatic representation of the 'Levels of Use' described above, see Figure 4.1.

Finally, irrespective of the approach taken, the aim of using the EFQM Excellence Model is to improve healthcare delivery and realise tangible benefits. This in mind, Chapter 5 provides some indication of the benefits and improvements already demonstrated in a number of healthcare environments.

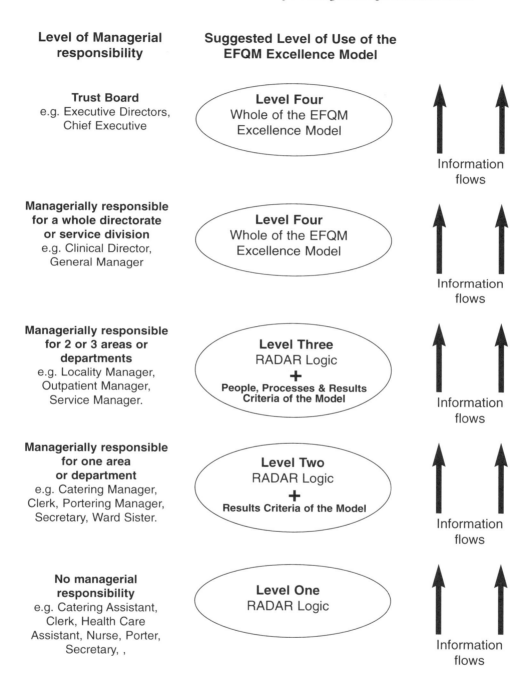

**Figure 4.1  Suggested Levels of Use of the EFQM Excellence Model within healthcare**

# Chapter 5
# Benefits associated with
# using the EFQM Excellence
# Model within healthcare

### A need to know
All healthcare personnel irrespective of their role within the service are keen to know of the benefits associated with the EFQM Excellence Model before they embark upon the journey. Consequently anyone who is promoting or supporting the use of the Model within healthcare needs to be familiar with the benefits that have so far been attained. Whilst chapter 5 does not contain a definitive list it does provide a flavour of the diversity of the *sustainable* benefits gained through using the Model. The reader will note that only an indication of the benefits described in the book '*The Excellence Model in the Health Sector; Sharing good practice.*' (Stahr et al 2000) is given, in order that duplication is avoided.

### Benefits attained by specific healthcare organisations
### Salford Royal Hospitals NHS Trust
Salford Royal Hospitals NHS Trust (SRHT) realised a number of benefits from using the EFQM Excellence Model especially in areas where there was good leadership. One of the examples given was in the area of diabetes. To illustrate the percentage of patients screened annually rose from 55% in 1993 to 73% in 1998 and the percentage of patients whose cholesterol levels were <5.5mmol rose from 32% in 1993 to 74% in 1998 (Key Performance Indicators). These are significant achievements when at the beginning of the excellence journey the department was experiencing serious problems manifested by an increasing number of complaints from patients.

More broadly, through the commitment and drive of the Chief Executive and whole Trust Board the ongoing efforts towards excellence have celebrated over 160 significant healthcare improvements for the customers, people and stakeholders of SRHT. Evidence of these improvements can be found on the Trust's intranet where details are stored following the quarterly Trust Quality Award ceremonies (Key Performance Indicators). Holding the details of improvement projects on the intranet supports the sharing of best practice and stimulates others to strive for continuous improvement in the service that they deliver.

In line with the principle of continuous improvement, SRHT are still realising benefits from using the EFQM Excellence Model. To illustrate, in January 2001 a significant achievement was realised in the pharmacy department from applying the RADAR logic to 'discharge prescription completion times'. The effect was a reduction in the time taken to prepare discharge prescriptions from an average of 77 minutes to 46 minutes and work is still underway to further improve this turnaround time.

## South Tees Acute Hospitals Trust

Following one self-assessment exercise at STAHT it became evident that an area for improvement was the timeliness of thank you rewards and the feeling amongst staff that the rewards were not genuine. As a result the Leadership Steering Group undertook a review and came up with a number of recommendations, which included encouraging a climate of recognition, an improved Thank You Award Scheme and a Trust Team of the Year Award. All the recommendations from the group were actioned and a subsequent self-assessment demonstrated a 7% increase in the number of staff who felt valued by their manager (People Results).

The Division of Women and Children were so enthused by the corporate drive for excellence that despite exceeding all national standards for colposcopy, the team still felt there was room for improvement. Armed with this belief and energy a number of process changes within the colposcopy clinic were implemented. The effect was a reduction in the *did not attend* rates from 20% to 10%, a reduction in the time taken to generate appointments from 13.5 days to 24 hours, and a reduction in the unnecessary smear rate by 100% (Customer Results).

However, one of the most significant benefits achieved by STAHT is that *all* areas of the Trust are *actively* involved in improvement activities towards developing healthcare excellence.

## Wakefield and Pontefract Community Health NHS Trust

Wakefield and Pontefract Community Health NHS Trust (WPCHT) found that using the EFQM Excellence Model not only changed what they did but also the way they thought about things. A corporate benefit attained from the first self-assessment was clarity around the organisation's customer base. This seems basic but the demands of healthcare often mean that there is little time to reflect and recognise the incremental changes that have taken place over the years. Because using the EFQM Excellence Model involves organisations self-assessing against a comprehensive framework a necessary first step is often defining who the organisation's customers, people and stakeholders are. In undertaking the first step the corporate team of the Trust found they could better agree and balance their portfolio of services for meeting the differing needs of customers, people and stakeholders (Policy and Strategy).

A further benefit described is that achieved by the district nurse team who reduced the incidence of pressure sores by 50% an achievement that is still being sustained (Customer Results). The approach involved identifying patients at risk of developing pressure sores and taking appropriate preventative action. WPCHT examples illustrate that benefits can be attained at both strategic and operational levels.

Similar to Salford and South Tees, Wakefield and Pontefract observed that using the EFQM Excellence Model stimulated the involvement of many people within the organisation to take positive action towards excellence.

## A district general hospital providing acute and community services

Despite the organisation not attaining success as a whole with using the EFQM Excellence Model, significant benefits were seen within one department enthusiastic in its use. The journey began with a two-day workshop when the department compared itself to 'best in class'. During the comparison phase the departmental team recognised they had many strengths, but many, if not more 'major weaknesses', the latter of which included having no: -

- agreed vision, (Leadership)
- consistency of generic practices i.e. processes for collecting management information, incident reporting, and complaints handling, (Processes)
- generic appraisal, recruitment or induction processes, (People)
- customer focus. (Customers)

With the aid of self-assessment and immense personal commitment and hard work, a lot was achieved during the 5 years the department used the Model. For instance, staff gained a sense of corporate identity, an outward looking approach, and an appreciation of the contribution the whole trust made towards the delivery of healthcare locally, regionally and nationally. Additionally, because the sub-directorate remained steadfast in its pursuit of continuous improvement, it attained a high profile within the trust, and in some instances was able to demonstrate and share 'best' practices.

By putting the customer first, a visible change in culture emerged. For instance, staff no longer concentrated on empire building. Instead they saw each service as being equal irrespective of its whole time equivalent make up (i.e. more physiotherapists to podiatrists and speech and language therapists). This engendered a feeling of teamwork, support and empowerment. Staff also recognised the importance of their contribution, which resulted in increased flexibility and innovation when striving for improving the experience and satisfaction of customers. (Jackson et al 1998)

Further tangible benefits included a common understanding and a positive approach to problem solving. In terms of performance measurement, the department demonstrated more efficiency as;
- generic practices and improved referral systems reduced duplication and unnecessary patient contacts (Processes),
- there was an emphasis on getting things *right first time* (Processes), AND
- data collection processes were more streamlined (Partnerships and Resources).

What should be noted here though is that it took five years to get to this particular part of the journey.

## A rural maternity unit

Irrespective of the lack of success regarding sustainability for using the Model, some benefits were attained in the rural maternity unit. In particular, utilising the EFQM Excellence Model as a mechanism for delivering clinical governance enabled midwifery managers to appreciate the similarities between the two concepts. Prior to using the EFQM Excellence Model, the approach towards clinical governance was fragmented. Initiatives like; journal clubs, one-off audits and customer surveys were being implemented in the absence of a holistic plan and a framework for regular review (Leadership). Utilising the Model proved particularly advantageous for addressing these specific issues. The result was a clear sense of direction and an appreciation of the unit's strengths and areas for improvement (Leadership).

It also became evident that using the EFQM Excellence Model had the potential to influence the norms and values associated with the organisational culture. Similar to the district general hospital, the senior management team began to recognise that they had been working without a clear vision, targets or a sound performance measurement system. Insights began to change and behaviours followed. For instance, managers recognised that in the main they devised and executed plans but never identified a review and improvement process. An example was the rotation of midwives within the maternity unit (People).

Secondly, target setting was not a feature associated with the day to day running of the unit until the principles of the EFQM Excellence Model were adopted. The team became more aware of the value of performance measurement and management in the pursuit of clinical governance and excellence. Utilising the model also challenged traditional ways of working. For instance the team were required to examine their; leadership style, involvement with customers and their commitment and actions towards quality. Clearly this was uncomfortable at times and led to features associated with resistance to change. Øvretveit (1999) observed similar characteristics in his study and therefore recommended that leaders should not fight resistance but work with it through understanding and dialogue. Furthermore, Øvretveit (1999) maintained that leaders should expect and welcome opposition as no resistance meant managers' had failed to really understand the process.

## Lockside Medical Centre (A small general practice)

Despite having an established culture within the practice, whereby everyone wanted to deliver an excellent service and take positive steps towards that, the EFQM Excellence Model did add value. As a demonstration of this, the interview aspect of the process highlighted the issues that were important to the organisation's people. Previous to that the issues were not as openly discussed. Following on from the interviews, a questionnaire was designed to form the basis of the People perception element of the EFQM Excellence Model and a positive feeling about the process could be felt throughout the whole practice.

There was so much enthusiasm for securing improvements that the clerical and secretarial team began to collect data on their 'headless chickens'. Headless chickens were described as irritants in the practice that involved rework, chasing up information in response to enquiries, or other activities deemed as wasting valuable time (Processes). Within eleven days of commencing the exercise, corrective actions were put in place for the most common 'headless chickens' and improvements in the service realised. Table 5.1 contains a summary of the incidents and improvement actions taken.

| Incident | Frequency | Action taken |
|---|---|---|
| Booking an ambulance. Sometimes efforts were duplicated because there was no record of whether or not a fax had been sent to the ambulance service | 3 | Staff agreed to put a date in the communication book when they had faxed ambulance control and to tick the book when confirmation received. Unnecessary chasing up in response to patient enquiries ceased. |
| Contacting pharmacists to chase up prescriptions | 8 | Lists were prepared for each pharmacist so the team knew if the prescriptions had been collected. Everyone made sure that the pharmacists had the relevant prescriptions before the patient was due to collect the medication. Unnecessary chasing up ceased. |
| Medical records missing | 6 | More emphasis was placed on using the tracer cards |
| Criteria about new patients wishing to register | 3 | The criteria were not clear, so a letter was typed to explain the criteria to patients wishing to register with the practice, thereby achieving service improvements. |

**Table 5.1  Summary of incidents and improvement actions taken**

As a result of the self-assessment process, the general practitioners undertook a literature review to determine which treatment interventions were the most effective. The findings from the exercise identified that in total seven general practice treatments and/or interventions were associated with saving the most lives. Furthermore, if the practice adopted these treatments and/or interventions 30 mortalities could be avoided each year (Key Performance Outcomes). Consequently steps were taken to ensure that the necessary treatments and/or interventions were included in the practices portfolio of services (Policy and Strategy, Partnerships and Resources, Processes).

## Burton Hospitals

Despite only using the Model for approximately ten months (at the time of writing) Burton Hospitals achieved some significant benefits in that initial phase. For instance, efforts to improve teamworking were stimulated and information sharing enhanced. To demonstrate one team undertook their self-assessment for the Chief Executive Review during which time there were some people who actively supported the process and some who passively resisted it. Consequently, when the review was taking place some of the team members were not aware of the contents of the self-assessment, thereby oblivious to the key enablers and results for their own department.

As a result queries and comments were raised which highlighted the lack of teamworking, a factor that the team were uncomfortable with and wanted to address. To illustrate this, one of the consultants said '*I used to prefer it when the social worker used to do a ward round*', the senior nurse responded with '*She still does!*' That evening the senior team met up at the house of one of the member's and an approach to improve teamwork was agreed. A further feature of that review was a discussion around who needed departmental information and why they may have needed it. Prior to the review information was not shared as widely as it could have been which had a detrimental effect on the team's performance. However, the situation is now much improved.

Within the ten months the Chief Executive had held twenty-two reviews from which improvement plans were agreed and corrective actions commenced. Additionally, the Chief Executive's knowledge of the values, efforts and strife's of the organisation's people was greatly enhanced (Leadership). Furthermore, despite a purposeful lack of formal training, the experience enabled the Chief Executive to easily differentiate between enablers and results and therefore become very results focused, a challenge for many healthcare professionals.

The Executive team also found that the EFQM Excellence Model was robust and flexible enough to integrate any previous or new initiatives. For instance during an away day it was identified that the Model could easily accommodate the enablers and results within the NHS plan, thereby providing a consistent approach for delivering a new directive.

Another department within Burton Hospitals identified a particularly good approach for developing the results focus that healthcare so often struggles with. The approach involved preparing a process flow chart for significant clinical processes. At certain steps of the process the team ensured that they determined the result they anticipated from the action documented. Hence, if a patient were to receive a certain intervention or element of care (nursing, medical or otherwise) the team would identify what that intervention or care was hoping to achieve. Once the desired achievements were identified the team were able to set up systems to measure performance in relation to results as well as enablers.

The above descriptions are not exhaustive in terms of the benefits that Burton Hospitals attained in the first ten months but they do provide some indication of the value-adding potential of using the EFQM Excellence Model within healthcare.

## Generic benefits

Given the comprehensive nature of the EFQM Excellence Model the demands for accurate, timely and easily accessible information are never ending. Additionally, the information needs to be available to anyone within the organisation who feels they have a need for it, thereby putting increasing demands on the systems to collect data which in the first instance many need to be undertaken manually. Consequently some would view this as a negative in relation to using the Model. However, in reality the self-assessment framework informs the development of information systems thereby ensuring that the organisation collects data that is useful to both clinicians and managers.

Gone are the days when the information technology (IT) department informs clinicians and managers what can be delivered. Instead the opposite occurs which is a situation that IT departments have been trying to achieve for sometime. Furthermore the self-assessment process required for the Chief Executive Reviews highlights areas whereby duplicate efforts are being deployed around data collection. Once the duplications have been identified efforts are often focused on agreeing a 'one stop shop' for gathering the information required.

A further benefit that has been mirrored in a number of organisations is the sharing of values and priorities amongst clinical and non-clinical departments. In particular by attending the Chief Executive Reviews contract and planning directors have been informed of the developments in clinical practice. As a consequence, contracting negotiations have improved because they are not solely relying on past performance trend data. Rather they are kept up to date with clinical developments. Secondly, finance directors become aware of the aspirations of clinicians and clinicians appreciate the constraints and efforts of the finance department. Whilst it does not always solve problems it does support teamworking and a feeling that everyone is working towards the same goal.

Many organisations and departments using the EFQM Excellence Model express how valuable the process has been for determining priorities, agreeing a vision and focusing efforts on achieving that vision. By undertaking a self-assessment and determining targets the organisation and/or department is able to clearly identify gaps and agree which areas need to be addressed and in what order. Nevertheless, the most significant benefit for healthcare has been the cultural shift from being enabler focused to being results focused, a factor, which is crucial for pursing excellence.

## Moving from an enabler to a results focus

Within healthcare there is a real focus on enablers, which means that in the main measurement systems are designed around process measures rather than outcome measures. A reason for this may be that, in the past, governments have tended to be more interested in process measures than health outcomes or other healthcare results. Examples of process measures are waiting lists, cancelled operations, length of stay and length of wait for emergency admission through Accident and Emergency. In relation to adopting the principles of excellence the aforementioned measures are clearly a means to an end. For instance by shortening the waiting lists (Processes enabler) an assumption is made that this improves health outcomes (Key Performance Results) and patient satisfaction (Customer Result).

If healthcare organisations concentrate on measuring, monitoring and improving a process, but fail to measure, monitor and understand the impact of that process improvement on health outcome and patient satisfaction then it is not subscribing to the principles of excellence. Given that the EFQM Excellence Model assigns equal weighting of 50% to enablers and 50% to results, this then implies that similar improvement efforts need to be applied to both, otherwise the organisation can never attain excellence.

Reaching this level of thinking is one of the most significant benefits that the EFQM Excellence Model has delivered for healthcare. In essence the EFQM Excellence Model has widened healthcare organisations from being primarily enabler focused to being both enabler and results focused. However, this has not been an easy journey for healthcare and organisations embarking upon using the Model have experienced more difficulty with this aspect than anything else. In view of this, examples of healthcare results that are actually used in practice are given below.

In some cases examples of enablers that have been mistaken for results areas in the first instance are also given, so as to further demonstrate the difference between the two. Where the examples do not contain a list of enablers that are commonly mistaken for results it can be attributed to the level of input provided by the expert facilitator. Hence, the expert facilitator was able to ensure that the first hurdle was bypassed rather than overcome. Similarly, the intention of providing the following examples of results is to enable healthcare personnel embarking upon using the EFQM Excellence Model to avoid that first hurdle.

The reader must note that the suggested results areas below are by no means a definitive list, prescriptive or indicative that a healthcare organisation will attain excellence by adopting all, most, some or any of them. Rather they are real life examples which healthcare personnel may choose to utilise. Alternatively, the examples may stimulate teams to determine results areas appropriate for their department. With regards to departments delivering direct patient care, clinical governance should also support the process for identifying key clinical results areas.

In some cases it will be noted that experience to date has only identified a small number of Key Performance Results in some healthcare departments, especially in comparison to others. The main factor influencing the number of Key Performance Results identified is whether performance measures have been a long-term feature of the department or not. In the event of the latter, only a small number of results are suggested so as to reaffirm the message that users embarking upon the EFQM Excellence Model should ensure that they do not '*bite off more than they can chew*'. It is better to start doing a few things well and then grow, than to try and do a lot of things not so well in the first instance which will be detrimental to the long-term success of striving for excellence. Particularly as the 'must-do' results areas will still need to be delivered alongside the desirables.

A further factor worthy to note here is that for any result area identified as important enough to ascribe the EFQM Excellence Model principles and rigour to, the team (organisational or departmental) need to demonstrate:

- positive trends and/or sustained good performance,
- performance that reflects appropriate targets,
- performance that compares well with other organisations,
- results are caused by the enablers (actions), and
- the scope of the results address relevant areas. (EFQM 1999a)

## Example results areas for Customers

### Perceptions

Results from undertaking patient satisfaction surveys, focus groups and other perception data collection methods. Some healthcare examples of perception measures include percentage of patients who are happy with:

- Day, date and time of appointment
- General Practitioner's diagnosis
- Consultation time with General Practitioner
- Consultant's diagnosis
- Consultation time with Consultant
- Treatment choices
- Actual treatment
- Continuity
- Confidentiality of the service
- Pain relief
- The information received
- Communications
- Length of time waiting for someone to answer the telephone
- The environment (cleanliness etc)
- Sign posting
- Car parking
- Transport arrangements
- Catering
- Complaints handling
- Friendliness of staff (could segment against staff groups)

Results from undertaking internal customer surveys, focus groups and other perception data collection methods. Some healthcare examples of perception measures include percentage of internal customers who are happy with:

- Turn around times from requesting X-ray to procedure being performed
- Turn around times for reporting haematology results
- Accuracy rate for test results
- Service from help desk
- Information regarding maintenance jobs outstanding
- Length of time waiting for someone to answer the telephone
- Security
- Clarity of finance reports
- Accuracy of finance reports

- Clarity of performance reports
- Accuracy of performance reports

## Indicators – External Customers

*These healthcare measures are internal ones used by the organisation to monitor, understand, predict and improve performance and to predict external customer perceptions.*

- Proportion of patients who experience cancelled planned treatments
- Proportion of patients who experience cancelled outpatient appointments
- Percentage of patients waiting < 26 weeks for outpatient appointment
- Percentage of patients waiting > 26 weeks for outpatient appointment
- Percentage of patients seen within 30 minutes of appointment time in outpatients
- *Did not attend* rates
- Number of requests for appointment times that are outside the current norm
- Percentage of discharge plans adhered to
- Average number of times telephone rings before it is answered
- Pain scores
- Number of aggressive incidents
- Number of complaints from patients
- Turnaround times for resolving complaints
- Percentage of patient complaints progressing to Independent Review
- Number of car parking spaces for patients and their relatives
- Percentage of contracts renewed
- Percentage of contracts lost
- Number of new contracts
- Ratio for number of customer needs identified against customer needs met
- Percentage of complaints resulting in improvement actions
- Number of improvement suggestions
- Number of verbal compliments
- Number of written compliments

## Indicators – Internal Customers

*These healthcare measures are internal ones used by the organisation to monitor, understand, predict and improve performance and to predict internal customer perceptions.*

- Number of complaints
- Number of compliments
- Percentage of complaints resulting in improvement actions
- Number of improvement suggestions

- Length of time from request to completion of request (maintenance, IT support, laboratory services, X-ray, domestic, catering etc)
- Accuracy rate for reporting on tests
- Feedback rates for documents circulated for consultation
- Product returns to supplies
- Number of repeated request for jobs outstanding

*Example results areas for People*

Perceptions

*Results from undertaking people satisfaction surveys, focus groups and other perception data collection methods. Some healthcare examples of perception measures include percentage of people who are happy with:*

- Working at the organisation
- Support in the workplace
- The management team
- The management of change
- Recognition from manager
- Feeling of being valued
- Feeling able to do a good job
- Roles and responsibilities
- Team atmosphere
- Personal contribution to overall team
- Being encouraged to put forward suggestions for improvement
- Pay
- Job security
- Being treated fairly
- The information to do their job
- Communications
- Their knowledge and understanding of the organisation's mission, vision and values
- The organisation's commitment to it's employees
- Balancing work and family commitments
- Annual leave booking system
- Amount of time to do the job required
- Induction programme (corporate and departmental)
- Time allocated for study
- Appraisal system
- Training and development opportunities
- Usefulness of training opportunities
- Access to information technology systems
- Information technology systems

Indicators

*These healthcare measures are internal ones used to monitor, understand, predict and improve the performance of the organisation's people and to predict their perceptions.*

- Percentage of staff covered by Investors in People accreditation
- Percentage of staff with personal development plans
- Number of training opportunities available
- Range of training opportunities available
- Average training days taken
- Did not attend rates for training and development opportunities
- Training budget as a percentage of total staff costs
- Hours of overtime worked
- Number of suggestions for improvement actions
- Percentage of staff involved in departmental self-assessment
- Percentage of staff receiving face to face team briefing
- Number of staff accidents in the workplace
- Number of occasions of violence, physical abuse or verbal abuse against staff
- Vacancy rates
- Average length of time taken to recruit to posts
- Retention rates
- Percentage of leavers who attend staff exit interview
- Percentage of long service awards
- Average age of workforce
- Percentage of staff in NHS pension scheme
- Percentage of sickness absence
- Percentage of staff undergoing return to work interviews following sickness absence
- Percentage of new starters who have attended corporate induction
- Percentage of staff who in past 12 months have attended mandatory training
- Percentage of junior medical posts achieving New Deal Targets
- Number of nurse bank hours used
- Number of annual leave requests turned down
- Grade mix of all staff

## Example results areas for Society

Perceptions

*Results from undertaking society satisfaction surveys, public meetings and seeking views from public representatives. Some healthcare examples of perception measures include percentage of society who is happy with:*

- Information received regarding capital development projects
- Opportunities to put forward views regarding capital development projects

- Opportunities to influence capital development projects
- Noise levels (probably more relevant with siren use of ambulance services)
- Pollution emissions

Indicators

*These healthcare measures are the internal ones used to monitor, understand, predict and improve the performance of the organisation and to predict the perceptions of society.*

- Number of times a member of society makes contact to make a positive comment
- Number of times a member of society makes contact to make a negative comment
- Ratio of positive to negative media coverage
- Number of awards received
- Number of new services/treatments launched
- Number of products recycled
- Number of visits to schools
- Average mileage for community services

## Example Key Performance Results for Accident and Emergency

Outcomes

Indicators

- Door to needle time (compare during office hours and out of office hours)
- Average length of time patients wait to see a doctor (compare during office hours and out of office hours)
- Missed fracture rate
- Transit time for patients with fractured neck of femur
- Unscheduled patient return rate
- Average trolley waits
- Percentage of patients' triaged

## Example Key Performance Results for Anaesthetics

Outcomes

- Recovery time for patients on Sevoflurane versus other drugs
- Percentage of patients booked for day surgery who are not suitable on the day

Indicators
- Percentage of lists which start on time
- Percentage of day surgery lists that are performed by consultants
- Percentage of patients who have a pre-op assessment

### Example Key Performance Results for Capital Development
Outcomes
- Percentage of projects on financial target
- Percentage of projects on time target
- Percentage of projects meeting benefits realisation

Indicators
- Accuracy rate for project briefs
- Ratio of tendered to negotiated contracts
- Expenditure on outside management/project consultants
- Number of variations per contract

### Example Key Performance Results for Cardiology
Outcomes
- Mortality rates

Indicators
- Percentage of eligible patients who should receive thrombolysis and do
- Speed within which patients suffering from chest pain are assessed on arrival
- Speed within which eligible patients receive thrombolysis
- Percentage of patients who have their lipid levels checked following discharge
- Percentage of patients receiving aspirin following discharge
- Percentage of patients receiving beta-blockers following discharge
- Average wait for an angiograph list

### Example Key Performance Results for Chaplaincy (identified through workshop not seen in use at time of writing)
Outcomes
At time of writing main outcomes related to customer and people (chaplaincy team) results. Customers were seen as patients, their relatives and staff (internal customers).

Indicators
- Total number of requests for chaplaincy services
- Time from request for chaplaincy services to provision

- Percentage of requests accommodated
- Average attendance at services
- Number of hits on website

### Example Key Performance Results for Chemical Pathology
Outcomes

- Percentage of patients who receive primary intervention for high cholesterol levels whose level reaches 5.2
- Percentage of patients who receive secondary intervention for high cholesterol levels whose level reaches 5.2
- Accuracy of Downs screening
- Number of pathology discoveries

Indicators

- Patients who have lipid estimation within ten minutes of appointment time
- Referral rate
- Percentage of letters dictated within same day of clinic visit
- Percentage of General Practitioner's (GP) who receive letters within 4 days of patient visiting clinic
- Funding from clinical trials

### Example Key Performance Results for Clinical Support Services
Outcomes

- Proportion of services demonstrating positive trends for clinical performance
- Budget variance

Indicators

- Number of changes in practice as a result of clinical evidence
- Number of improvement projects completed
- Number of publications in peer reviewed journals
- Number of publications in non-peer reviewed journals
- Number of presentations at conferences
- Turnaround time from request to result reporting
- Prescribing costs
- Income
- Endowment income
- Cost Improvement Programme variance
- Number of research and development projects
- Percentage of research and development projects on target
- Number of adverse incidents

### *Example Key Performance Results for Community*

Outcomes
- Percentage of patients who achieved their therapeutic goals
- Success rates for treatments
- Budget variance

Indicators
- Waiting times for services (Podiatry, Speech therapy, Physiotherapy etc)
- Percentage of inappropriate referrals received
- Percentage of ineffectual visits
- Percentage of first visits to patients discharged from hospital resulting in readmission
- Percentage of patients on caseloads who have achieved their therapeutic goals and continue to be seen because there is no other acceptable alternative
- Percentage of patients discharged from inpatient care with an appropriate discharge plan
- Percentage of admissions prevented by the Rapid Response Team
- Average response times for Rapid Response Team
- Percentage of needs identified by Health Visitors which are unmet
- Average turnaround time from admission to discharge from caseload
- Attendance rates for clinics
- Average mileage per visit
- Number of security incidents

### *Example Key Performance Results for Critical Care* (Intensive Care Unit)

Outcomes
- Mortality rates
- Number of unpredictable cardiac arrests

Indicators
- Percentage of admissions refused
- Transfers to other Critical Care Units due to lack of beds
- Nosocomal infection rates
- Number of patients scoring high on Early Warning Score for cardiac arrests where appropriate action was not taken
- Number of patients not enrolled onto Early Warning Score programme who should have been
- Percentage of elective cases cancelled
- Percentage of discharges delayed
- Percentage of premature discharges

### *Example Key Performance Results for Dermatology*

Outcomes

- Completeness rates for excision of basal cell carcinomas
- Mortality rates for patients with melanomas
- Mortality rates for patients with bullous pemphigoid
- Percentage improvement after 6 months on Psoriasis Symptom Management Programme

Indicators

- Average waiting time for Cancer diagnosis

### *Example Key Performance Results for Diabetes*

Outcomes

- Limb amputation rate
- Percentage of patients with diabetic retinopathy
- Percentage of patients with end stage renal failure
- Mortality rate from coronary heart disease
- New blindness rates

Indicators

- Percentage of patients receiving an annual review
- Waiting times
- Readmission rates for patients with ketoacidosis
- Compliance rate with preparation for surgery regime
- Percentage of patients who receive appropriate treatment post infarction
- Number of podiatry visits
- Ratio for percentage of patients who should be on insulin and who are on insulin
- Average length of hospital stay for patients with diabetes
- Average healing time for ulcers (segmented by treatments)
- Percentage of patients receiving appropriate follow-up

### *Example Key Performance Results for Elderly*

Outcomes

- Mortality Rate
- Functional levels on admission compared to discharge

Indicators

- Actual v planned activity

- Average length of stay segmented by consultant
- Percentage of appropriate admissions
- Readmission rates
- Rate of day cases
- Domiciliary attendance rate
- Speed of access from diagnosis to intervention
- Average time between assessments
- Number of administration of medicine errors
- Average nutritional assessment scores
- Pressure sore rate

## *Example Key Performance Results for Ear, Nose and Throat (ENT)*
Outcomes
- Effectiveness rates for myrngoplasty
- Hearing Improvement scores following ear operation
- Survival rates for cancer

Indicators
- Percentage of note keeping that complies with standard
- Percentage of cancelled operations due to patient not being clinically fit on day of operation
- Percentage of discharge letters received by GP within 7 days of patient discharge
- Average length of time to provide a hearing aid
- Average time taken from referral to definitive treatment for cancer patients

## *Example Key Performance Results for Facilities*
Outcomes
- Budget balance variance
- Percentage of space utilised
- Functional suitability
- Energy efficiency
- Variance rate for legal maintenance requirements
- Variance rate for fire maintenance requirements
- Variance rate for Health and Safety maintenance requirements
- Number of security incidents
- Compliance with clinical waste legislation

Indicators
- Income from car parking

- Average time taken from request to completion of maintenance work
- Response times from requests to jobs completed
- Percentage of jobs completed right first time
- Cost of food wastage
- Cost of disposing clinical waste

## *Example Key Performance Results for Finance and Information*

Outcomes

- Budget variance
- External Financing Limit
- Return on Capital Employed
- Capital
- Number of eighteen month waits
- Percentage of patients waiting >26 weeks for an Outpatient appointment
- Percentage of patients waiting <13 weeks for an Outpatient appointment
- Average length of stay
- Did not attend rates

Indicators

- Accuracy rate of predictions
- Cost Improvement Programme variance
- Percentage of time met deadline for distributing finance reports
- Percentage of time met deadline for distributing information reports
- Accuracy level of budgetary information reports
- Number of budget statement queries
- Percentage of suppliers paid within 30 days
- Percentage of debt received on time
- Average number of days taken to collect payment from private patients
- Interest Revenue
- Rate of return on Trust funds
- Compliance with internal audit recommendations
- Percentage for medical records being available when required
- Percentage for medical records being in the right place
- Number of liability claims not covered by insurance
- Number of payroll enquiries
- Number of inappropriate reminders to debtors
- Accuracy rate for monthly forecasts
- Commercial bank account balance
- Hit rate for clinical coding

- Number of information technology system breakdowns
- Average length of time for help/enquiry desk to answer the telephone
- Average time interval from providing advice/support to seeing improvements in financial management

Examples of enablers incorrectly viewed as results
- Revenue and capital budgets agreed by Board
- Produce Corporate Financial Proformas for Region
- Distribute charitable monies reports to fund manager quarterly

## Example Key Performance Results for General Practice

Outcomes
- Number of asthma admissions (for patients known to have asthma)
- Number of myocardial infarctions
- Number of premature deaths
- Smoking cessation rates
- Unplanned teenage pregnancy rate
- Net profit on income as a percentage

Indicators
- Number of new diagnoses of cancer
- Number of serious diagnostic errors
- Take up rates for effective interventions (to patients at risk of death or disability who have been diagnosed with coronary heart disease risk factors, atrial fibrillation, established coronary heart disease, diabetes, serious mental illness, chest disease, pregnancy or childhood illnesses)
- Percentage of patients known to have diabetes who have a HbA1c of <7
- Take up rates for review (by patients taking dangerous medication, for instance non-steroidal anti-inflammatories in the elderly, Lithium, Warfarin, Methotrexate, Sulphasalazine)
- Percentage of prescriptions 'cashed in'
- Percentage take up of vaccinations
- Number of iatrogenic incidences
- Number of appointment errors
- Number of prescription errors
- Number of times medical records are missing
- Percentage of smears that are inadequate
- Number of incorrectly completed blood test forms
- Number of referrals 'going astray'
- Time taken for computer support to rectify problem or fault
- Number of 'improved' processes

- Payments per patient
- Items of Service claims per patient
- Percentage of staff wages reimbursed
- Percentage of profit on items dispensed by practice
- Prescribing costs

### Example Key Performance Results for Genito-Urinary Medicine

Outcomes

Indicators

- Turnaround time for chlamydia test results
- Percentage of 'missed' chlamydia cases due to unsuitability of tests
- Percentage chlamydia tests repeated
- Percentage of epidemiological treatments for suspected chlamydia
- Percentage of routine appointments available within one week limit
- Percentage of emergency appointments available within same day or <24 hours
- Ratio of hospital to home based treatments for genital warts
- Percentage of contact slips returned
- Number of clinical risk forms for dispensing medication

### Example Key Performance Results for Haematology

Outcomes

Survival curves were given as a result but no detail was provided. In order to measure progress the result area needs to be very specific.

Indicators

- Percentage of unnecessary tests during service hours
- Percentage of unnecessary tests during out of hours
- Percentage of time that rapid response makes an impact on clinical management of care (out of hours)
- Percentage of time that rapid response makes an impact on clinical management of care (in service hours)
- Average cost of blood tests in service hours
- Average cost of blood tests out of service hours
- Percentage of incorrectly completed haematology request forms

### Example Key Performance Results for Human Resources

Outcomes

- Average length of long term sickness
- Staff retention rates

- Ethnicity workforce compared to corporate population
- Ethnicity workforce compared to catchment area
- Corporate sickness absence rates
- Gender mix
- Rate of unfilled posts
- Number of Employment Tribunal 1 cases
- Number of appeals heard by Chief Executive
- Budget variance

Indicators

- Average length of time for processing pre-employment questionnaire
- Average length of time to fill a vacancy
- Ratio of human resources staff to total organisation staff
- Average cost of advertising for vacant posts
- Average length of time for health clearance
- Ethnicity mix of responders to adverts
- Error rate for payroll
- Percentage of forms for payroll not completed correctly by managers
- Percentage of spend on outside courses
- Percentage of courses with long-term evaluation
- Did not attend rate for courses
- Percentage of training and development opportunities booked on-line
- Number of staff accidents
- Number of untoward incidents that involves >3 days sickness absence
- Number of reported bullying incidents
- Income (Occupational health, training and development etc)
- Percentage of training needs met
- Compliance rate for managers following guidelines

## *Example Key Performance Results for Medicine*

Outcomes

- Mortality rates
- 30 day hospital mortality rate following myocardial infarction
- Complication rates for patients with diabetes (loss of sight, amputations, foot ulcers etc)
- Budget variance

Indicators

- Percentage of patients discharged home within 56 days of emergency admission with a stroke
- Percentage availability of beds for admission

- Average waiting time for admission through Accident and Emergency
- Readmission rates
- Percentage of medical patients not on medical wards
- Delayed discharge rate
- Cost improvement plan variance

### *Example Key Performance Results for Mental health*

Outcomes

- Ratio for pre and post-treatment Anxiety and Depression scores
- Suicide rate
- Percentage of health promotion outcomes achieved
- Percentage of recommendations met from Mental Health Commission
- Accreditation from Royal College of Psychiatrists
- Budget variance

Indicators

- Percentage of National Service Framework standards being met
- Waiting times
- Did not attend rates
- Number of cancelled clinics
- Length of stay
- Bed occupancy
- Number of preventable readmissions
- Percentage of breakdown of placements
- Rates for non-compliance of medication
- Number of untoward incidents
- Use of atypical anti-psychotic medication
- Take up of non-medication therapies
- Take up of medication
- Ratio of appropriate to inappropriate referrals
- Number of corporate quality awards

### *Example Key Performance Results for Obstetrics and Gynaecology*

Outcomes

*Obstetrics*

- Maternal death rate
- Average birthweight
- Perinatal mortality rate
- Breastfeeding rates

Gynaecology

- Mortality rates for gynaecological patients

- Positive test rate following colposcopic treatment
- Cure rates for cancers

Fertility
- Success rates for secondary level interventions (Clomiphene therapy and Gonadotrophin therapy)
- Assisted conception success rates

Indicators

*Obstetrics*
- Teenage pregnancy rate
- Detection rate for fetal abnormality
- Percentage for induction of labour
- Caesarean section rate
- Average length of stay
- Number of third degree tears
- Number of unscheduled returns to theatre after delivering placenta and membranes
- Readmission rates within 28 days
- Number of visits for antenatal care
- Average number of post natal visits
- Antenatal admissions to antenatal ward
- Percentage of women who smoke who give up smoking during pregnancy
- Percentage of midwife deliveries
- Litigation costs

Gynaecology
- Biopsy rate for Colposcopy
- Misdiagnosed ectopic rates
- Unscheduled return to theatre after elective surgery
- Rate of post-operative complications
- Average length of stay

*Fertility*

Examples of enablers incorrectly viewed as results
- Percentage of times documentation meets audit requirement (this is a measure of the deployment of the documentation standard. The results would be what the standard was aiming to achieve.)

**Example Key Performance Results for Ophthalmology**

Outcomes
- Percentage of patients for which a reduction of stigmatism was achieved following surgery

- Comparison rates for pre-operative biometry with post-operative refraction
- Degeneration rate for patients with diabetes
- Cure rate for glaucoma

Indicators
- Surgical complication rates
- Ratio for day case and inpatient attendance
- Rate of inappropriate GP referrals
- Percentage of theatre slots left vacant
- Turnaround time for GP discharge letters
- Number of publications
- Research income

### Example Key Performance Results for Orthopaedics
Outcomes
- Mortality rate within 30 days of operation

Indicators
- Ratio of appropriate orthopaedic length of stay with actual length of stay
- Time from diagnosis of fractured femur to admission to orthopaedic ward
- Number of cancelled operations
- Average length of stay

### Example Key Performance Results for Outpatient Department
Outcomes
- Did not attend rates

Indicators
- Average length of wait in X-ray department
- Percentage for availability of medical records
- Length of time between request and receipt of medical records
- Error rate for correspondence and other documentation in medical records
- Average number of changes for appointment date and time

### Example Key Performance Results for Newborns and Paediatrics
Outcomes
- Success rates for treatment of retinopathy in premature infants
- Success rates for treatment interventions following intracranial sonography

- Success rates for treatment for congenital dislocation of the hip
- Success rates for treatment for urinary tract infection
- Mortality rates

Indicators
- Percentage of premature babies with retinopathy
- Percentage of neonatal retinopathy cases examined by ophthalmologist within recommended time frame
- Percentage of retinopathy cases receiving appropriate follow up
- Detection rate for congenital dislocation of the hip
- Percentage of babies receiving an intracranial sonography as per guideline. (The guideline is the enabler for this result.)
- Percentage of babies referred to neurosurgeon as per guidelines following intracranial sonography as per guideline. (The guidelines are the enabler for this result.)
- Percentage of readmissions of known diabetic children with a condition related to their diabetes
- Percentage of readmissions of known asthmatic children with a condition related to their asthma
- Number of older people having investigations following diagnosis of urinary tract infection
- Number of older people receiving appropriate treatment for conditions diagnosed following diagnosis of urinary tract infection
- Number of untoward incident reports
- Average length of stay following surgery
- Readmission rates
- Percentage of times requests for therapy support are accepted

## *Example Key Performance Results for Planning and Contracting*
Outcomes
- Performance variance
- Budget variance

Indicators
- Accuracy rate for action plans (time, finance and other variances)
- Percentage of bids for Regional funds which are successful
- Average number of meetings required for agreeing a contract
- Percentage of Clinical directors contributing to contracting process
- Average length of time from initial contract negotiations to signing off contracts

Examples of enablers incorrectly viewed as results
- Produce an annual business plan for the Trust
- Produce negotiated signed Service Level Agreements
- Produce accurate targets and monitoring data for all Directorates

## *Example Key Performance Results for Radiology*

Outcomes
- Compliance with Royal College of Radiologists guidelines
- Number of publications
- At time of writing Radiology were considering using three or four results from the national benchmarking tests

Indicators
- Appropriateness of requests for skull X-rays
- Appropriateness of requests for pre-operative chest X-rays
- Appropriateness of requests for trauma X-rays as requested by Accident and Emergency
- Average turnaround time for reporting
- Percentage of written reports for X-rays
- Accuracy rates for reporting
- Percentage of time radiographer is available on request
- Turnaround time for routine tests
- Turnaround time for urgent tests
- Turnaround time for inpatient tests
- Turnaround time for outpatient tests
- Turnaround time from dictation to report
- Income generated from maternity scan photographs
- Income and expenditure on medico-legal work
- Complication rate for lung biopsies
- Complication rate for liver biopsies
- Complication rate for oesophageal stents
- Complication rate for livery stents
- Complication rate for brain aneurysm coils
- Average dosage of radiation

## *Example Key Performance Results for Rehabilitation Services*

Outcomes
- Average Functional Assessment Scores (mobility, safety, non-reattendance)
- Post-operative chest infection rate
- Serum potassium levels in renal patients, following dietetic input
- Reduced episodes of foot ulceration

- Elderly Mobility Scale
- Level of independence in stroke patients (measured by Bartel Score)
- Percentage of patients demonstrating an improvement in range of movements from receiving hand therapy
- Budget variance

Indicators
- Average response time from request to delivery of assessment for treatment
- Average response time from assessing need for treatment to receipt of that treatment
- Mean healing time for foot ulceration
- Number of delayed discharges due to lack of rehabilitation therapy
- Continence rates

Examples of enablers incorrectly viewed as results
- Provision of a district wide Therapy Service
- Effective information sharing with all other Directorates
- Surgical podiatry triage

**Example Key Performance Results for Research and Development**

Outcomes
- Number of publications in peer reviewed journals
- Number of publications with an impact factor >1
- Number of non-medical publications
- Percentage of research findings being applied into practice
- Budget variance
- Number of research projects completed
- Number of adverse research incidents (governance)

Indicators
- Ratio of commercial to non-commercial funding
- Income
- Number of research projects on-going
- Percentage of projects related to NHS priorities
- Percentage of projects related to supercharged NHS priorities (Cancer, Cardiovascular disease, Stroke, Mental Health)
- Percentage of multi-disciplinary research projects
- Percentage of research projects with consumer involvement
- Grant application success rate

### *Example Key Performance Results for Rheumatology*
Outcomes
- Secondary fracture rates

Indicators
- Interval between onset of symptoms to referral
- Interval from referral to assessment in rheumatology clinic
- Proportion of 'positive' cases offered disease-modifying medication
- Proportion of 'positive' cases offered multidisciplinary package of care
- Proportion of at risk patients submitted for DEXA scanning
- Proportion of patients on treatment to prevent secondary fractures
- Proportion of (rheumatology) patients on prophylaxis against steroid induced Osteoporosis
- Percentage of patients on steroids alone
- Percentage of patients on steroids and other medication

### *Example Key Performance Results for Surgery*
Outcomes
- Cure rates
- 30 day mortality rate following surgery
- Survival rates for cancer

Indicators
- Compliance rate for administering thromboprophylaxis
- Compliance rate for administering prophylactic antibiotics
- Infection rates
- Transfer rates from key-hole to open surgery
- Length of stay
- Number of inappropriate admissions
- Theatre downtime
- Time between out-patient appointment to investigative/inpatient event
- Number of cancelled cancer investigative events
- Average time taken to find a bed for a patient
- Complication rate following surgery
- Number of peer-reviewed publications
- Number of non-peer reviewed publications
- Research income
- Number of presentations at conferences
- Average length of time between clinic visit and date of letter to patient
- Average length of time between clinic visit and date of letter to GP

Examples of enablers incorrectly viewed as results
- Number of partnership initiatives (this relates to deployment of an enabler, what needs to be identified here is what are the results that are aimed for by developing partnerships).
- Percentage of practice that is evidence-based (this relates to deployment of the enabler, what needs to be identified here is the clinical outcome expected from implementing each individual evidence-based practice).

### Example Key Performance Results for Urology
Outcomes
- Mortality rates following surgery

Indicators
- Readmission rates
- Percentage of patients with post-operative complications
- Length of stay following surgery

Examples of enablers incorrectly viewed as results
- Percentage of referrals aligning to the General Practitioner referral protocol for prostate cancer (this relates to measuring the deployment of this enabler)

Whilst the above does not cover all the areas of healthcare it does provide an insight into what constitutes a healthcare result. The reader may also note, that key performance indicators for some areas are key performance outcomes for others, this reflects the supportive role of some departments with regards to others.

### Did the EFQM Excellence Model really secure the benefits?
A question often raised during workshops is '*Did it really need the EFQM Excellence Model to deliver the improvements mentioned?*' Whilst the author would like to think that benefits could be secured irrespective of whether the EFQM Excellence Model is being used or not, regrettably this is does not appear to be the case. Hence, the answer most often given is in the form of a question '*If the benefit could have been realised without the EFQM Excellence Model, why was it not already being done?*' As yet no one has been able to answer the second question, which suggests that the EFQM Excellence Model is a suitable catalyst for the journey towards excellence. Furthermore, its whole systems approach means that it supports personnel to identify and address issues that cross traditional functional boundaries thereby promoting wider teamworking.

Finally, the Model has been shown to secure a *sustainable* drive towards continuous improvement and excellence. Even so, it is recognised that achieving this is very demanding and needs to be carefully implemented if the full benefits are to be realised. This is mind chapter 6 is dedicated to 'Making it Happen' and thus contains a number of tips and explanations for turning the myth of organisational excellence into a reality.

# Chapter 6
# Making it happen

**Believing in healthcare excellence**

Before the road towards excellence can be taken the drivers need to believe in their overall direction. Without the belief that the characteristics associated with healthcare excellence can be attained, there is no point taking the first step. However, in many cases seeing is synonymous with believing and seeing healthcare excellence is not so easy. Nevertheless, seeing excellence characteristics in other organisations is relatively easy and does result in a belief that excellence is attainable. Therefore visiting organisations that have won or achieved prize-winning status from applying for a national or European Quality Award is an extremely useful endeavour if people need to see before they can believe.

The statement comes from the experience of being an award assessor for the British Quality Foundation when the author was fortunate enough to assess an organisation that achieved prize-winning status. During the site visit when the assessment team spent a full week in the organisation, it became very clear that the characteristics of excellence permeated the whole establishment. So much so that the feeling amongst the team was that they had been '*transferred from the real world into a world of quality*'. Sounds a little twee, but the experience was so profound that it dispelled any doubt that excellence could be achieved in an organisation.

So what did the prize-winning organisation have that was so special? Well, it had leaders who were visibly committed towards the concepts of excellence and prepared to go that extra mile to achieve their vision. There was innovation, creativity and empowerment. Leaders encouraged the organisation's people to put forward suggestions for making things better and empowered them to see their ideas through. This feeling of involvement energised the whole organisation towards the same goal, the goal of excellence.

There was laughter, openness and teamwork. The assessment team regularly heard laughter from offices and the front line staff worked as comrades when new technology was introduced. To explain, the organisation's business to the lay person was delivering parcels, to the organisation it was '*solving people's problems*', and new technology was introduced whereby bar codes were used to register parcels prior to shipment. Recognising the similarity with supermarkets the warehouse staff jokingly put posters up at one of the bar code counters that said '10 items only' in a business that dealt with hundreds of thousands of parcels a day. The sense of wellbeing that the joke created helped the team to overcome the initial difficulties with the technology resulting in a positive working atmosphere. It gave the assessors a laugh too.

There was also wide sharing of information and energy for continuously improving anything and everything that people had an aspiration to improve. Because the leaders actively promoted doing things smarter, easier and better, a controlling culture was not a feature of this establishment. People were not afraid to question a process adopted by management, because they knew that a credible idea would be valued and put into practice if feasible. Consequently, a can-do attitude permeated the whole organisation, which was infectious and motivating. It was also managed because ideas still had to be considered in terms of their financial and other implications, but people recognised this and were involved in the process of determining whether or not a suggestion could be realistically adopted. Involving people in undertaking the investigative work associated with ideas supported learning amongst the workforce and enhanced the credibility of the improvement suggestions put forward. In some cases it also enabled people to seemingly do the impossible as when the idea was owned it was surprising what hurdles people would overcome to see their vision transformed into reality.

The development of the can-do attitude within the organisation was one of the most valuable messages that the assessment team took away with them because it was seen as a major contributor for achieving excellence. Therefore believing in excellence is synonymous with achieving it as the former invigorates a can-do attitude.

### Developing a can-do attitude

A can-do attitude is not a common feature within healthcare organisations, a view that stems from an extensive amount of interaction with professionals working in the field. To explain, whenever healthcare excellence is discussed the conversation invariably includes an element of why the vision cannot be achieved. Arguments like, *'Healthcare is different to business and so achieving excellence is more problematic'* or *'We couldn't do that you see because we have to deliver what the politicians want'* or *'Our service is different because each patient is an individual'* are often voiced. Hence some people spend more time explaining why they cannot deliver excellence than they do taking appropriate action towards it. A cannot-do attitude instead of a can-do attitude, prevails in some circumstances.

It could be argued that healthcare should have less difficulties than businesses do in delivering excellence because healthcare doesn't have to keep a distracting eye on surviving in a competitive market place. Furthermore, businesses similarly have to abide by legislation and .other constraints. For instance the parcel company mentioned earlier had extremely strict regulations put on it with regards to ensuring parcels did not contain anything illegal or dangerous. Meeting this legislative criterion at the same time as ensuring privacy for the customer's belongings was a particular sensitive issue that took time and could adversely impact on promises regarding delivery dates. Furthermore, customers expressed differing needs and demands that the company had to accommodate or risk losing business. Hence, people wanting parcels delivered had individual needs that challenged normal working practices just like patients. In addition, the company had to deal with achieving consistency of service in an organisation where the workforce spanned the whole of Europe, spoke different languages and had different cultural norms and working practices.

Achieving excellence is not easy in any organisation, which is why the can-do attitude is vital. There is no place for readily giving in to conceptual hurdles, rather the team need to spend their energies on identifying a way forward that will overcome the hurdle(s) in order that the organisation can progress towards excellence. Approaches like action learning sets have been shown to be very useful in healthcare for moving continuous improvement efforts forward and addressing particular complex issues.

Achieving an organisational 'can-do' attitude means that everyone needs to contribute towards making it happen and be prepared to go that extra mile. There are a number of quotes, which reflect this way of thinking;

*'Never doubt that a small group of thoughtful, committed people can change the world. Indeed, it is the only thing that ever has.'*

*'Attitude is a little thing that makes a big difference.'*

*'Don't wait for your ship to come in, swim out to it.'*

*'You cannot discover new oceans unless you have the courage to lose site of the shore.'*

Losing site of the shore in relation to healthcare excellence implies moving away from the 'tick box' approach to government initiatives and other demands. Therefore taking action involves more than collecting data or writing lengthy documents to indicate goals are being achieved when in reality nothing has changed. Making excellence happen involves changing day to day working practices for the benefit of the customers, people, society, governments and other stakeholders. It also involves collecting data to demonstrate the impact of those changed practices and being prepared to make further changes if the result isn't the one desired. The following quote from the Health Service Journal demonstrates how documents and information are often manipulated within healthcare to make it appear that an organisation is making progress rather than standing still, '*They tortured the statistics until they confessed*', (White 1999).

Hence, actions really do speak louder than words but taking action requires people to not only have a 'can do' attitude but also have the skills to make change happen. (McIntosh et al 2000) In relation to using the EFQM Excellence Model this requires people to fully understand the RADAR logic in order that they can strive for continuous improvement and ensure others join in the pursuit.

### Understanding RADAR

Despite delivering many workshops for healthcare professionals and applying continuous improvement to the presentation slides and accompanying dialogue, it has proved particularly challenging to explain the RADAR logic in an easily understandable manner, even though clinical and other healthcare examples have been used. However, recently it has been shown that understanding of the RADAR logic has greatly improved when the concept has been applied to dieting. Given this to be the case a practical guide for applying the EFQM Excellence Model within healthcare would not be complete unless the dieting example was included. By way of a reminder RADAR stands for:

- determine the desired **R**esults,
- plan and develop **A**pproaches,
- **D**eploy approaches and
- **A**ssess and **R**eview those approaches.

With regards to dieting the desired **R**esults may be to lose weight. However, losing weight is a loose term that may not stimulate continuous improvement. For instance if the person lost a kilogram then in effect that would mean they had lost weight and so the desired results would have been achieved. Although in reality everyone knows that a target of one kilogram is so easy to achieve that it isn't really a target. Hence the need to set appropriate targets which for some would be best done on a monthly basis and for others on a total end point basis.

To clarify, some people may be more motivated to lose weight if the target was three kilograms per month and others more motivated if it were twenty kilograms in total.

Setting targets in relation to aspirations and personal motivators implies ownership of how the Model concepts can be applied in practice, a healthy message to convey. For this example the target will be three kilograms per month. Targets may also be set in relation to what friends and others have achieved (benchmarks) so that there is a motivation to do better than one might have done had there been an absence of external stimuli. By way of a reminder, achieving excellence status in relation to the results criteria of the EFQM Excellence Model means that there needs to be a wide scope of results areas that demonstrate positive trends. In addition, performance needs to reflect appropriate targets and compare favourably with others and clarity around which enablers impacted on which results needs to be demonstrated.

Once the desired results have been clarified, the next step involves planning the Approaches. For losing weight the planned approaches may include having 1500 calories a day, going to the gym three times a week and having a lengthy walk every weekend. The analogy therefore is that often a number of approaches are required to achieve the desired result(s). Furthermore, an excellent approach is one where there is a clear rationale and a well defined, developed process.

Once the approaches have been planned then a systematic regime for implementing them needs to be Deployed (agreed and followed). With regards to the 1500 calorie diet, the dieter may need to go to the supermarket twice a week to ensure that fresh vegetables and fruit are continually available. The gym sessions may be best put into action if planned on certain days of the week, for example Mondays, Wednesdays and Fridays because the dieter has other commitments on Tuesdays and Thursdays. The weekend walk might be more likely to happen if a friend is involved and a suitable pair of walking boots and outdoor clothing made available. The analogy here is that ensuring the planned approaches happen requires integrated systems to be set up and necessary resources to be allocated. Consequently rigorous attention to detail is required for successfully implementing all planned approaches. Excellence in relation to deployment is assigned when the planned approach is implemented in a structured and systematic way.

Once deployment has been put into effect then it is time to undertake Assessment and Review. Assessment and review needs to look at three distinct elements, whether the approach was a suitable one, whether the approach was deployed and whether the desired results were achieved. In relation to determining whether or not the desired results have been achieved (lost three kilograms per month), undertaking assessment and review in this way identifies;

- sound approaches that have been deployed well, (this would be successful)
- sound approaches that have been deployed badly,
- poor approaches that have been deployed well, and
- poor approaches that have been deployed badly.

Excellence status for assessment and review is assigned when there is evidence of measurement, learning and improvement. Therefore, measures would need to be taken for the daily calorie intake; number of times went to the gym and had a walk on a weekend, and the monthly weight variance. In terms of learning, the dieter may discover that an odd chocolate fudge cake at the weekend had no detrimental effect on the desired results, or that the calorie intake was too high to achieve the target weight loss. Therefore evidence of improvement may include having chocolate fudge cake or some other treat once a week or alternatively altering the calorie intake to 1200 per day. Once the changes had been made assessment and review would need to be repeated at an appropriate juncture, in order that a cycle of continuous improvement was put into effect.

Some particularly useful analogies to come from the dieting example are that the dieter could have done everything by the book and still not lost weight. Similarly a healthcare team could have put great efforts into planning and deploying approaches for securing an improvement but have achieved much less than expected. Both situations would probably have a demotivating effect on the people concerned and yet if the results were still desired motivation could not wane, rather further efforts would be needed to achieve the identified goal. Alternatively the dieter could have cheated continuously and yet still achieved the desired result, not that this often happens in healthcare but sometimes little effort can be associated with substantial gains.

A second analogy relates to the difference between an enabler and a result. Is losing weight an enabler or a result? Because a measure can be assigned to the weight loss some would say it is a result and yet in real terms it is probably a *means* to an *end* thereby implying it is an enabler. In other words the end point may not be losing weight, it may be an increase in confidence, being able to fit into a certain outfit, or achieving a measured improvement in health like a reduction in blood pressure. Consequently desired measurable results (not enablers) with sound targets would need to be identified in order to apply the RADAR logic appropriately.

A third analogy is that the dieter needs to be very clear about the impact the enabler had on the result. Therefore the links between enablers and results would need to be explicit. As an explanation, the results the dieter (organisation) achieved would have been directly associated with the diet and exercise (enablers) applied and so if the dieter was not happy with the results, a change in the enablers would be required. The effect of those changes on the results would make it explicit how each approach impacted on the overall results.

All in all it can be seen that applying the RADAR logic is a rigorous process that has the potential to achieve desired results providing efforts are continuous and relentless, measurements are timely and appropriate, and learning opportunities are not overlooked. Furthermore, applying the RADAR logic to the nine criteria of the EFQM Excellence Model is a demanding exercise that requires a sensible implementation approach best achieved by starting simple.

## Starting simple

One of the most valuable lessons learned in healthcare was related to starting simple, not only in using the Model but also in applying energies towards improvement actions. In terms of using the Model starting simple meant applying the Model concepts and structure in an incremental way. A good approach involved identifying a few desired results areas first. The desired results areas included the must dos and those that related to eradicating irritants within the system, thereby supporting integration and avoiding using the Model as add on. Other desired results areas chosen were best if they related to the values and aspirations of the team. However, care needs to be exercised to ensure that a realistic number of results areas for applying continuous improvement actions to are chosen. Therefore, there is a requirement to sensitively balance enthusiasm with identifying desired results areas. Particularly when chapter 5 contains 63 example results areas for customers, 56 for people, 13 for society and an average of 13 per specialty for key performance, making up 145 results areas in total and that would be just the beginning. Obviously this number of results areas is far too much when wanting to apply a 'start simple' approach to using the Model. Hence a prioritisation process would need to be put into effect (see next section).

Once the desired results areas had been chosen, the next incremental step involved undertaking a self-assessment against the few desired results areas identified, which formed the basis of discussions at the Chief Executive Review. Starting simple also meant that people within the organisation did not strive for a perfect first self-assessment, instead the emphasis was put on '*getting the ball rolling*', learning together and making early tangible differences where possible.

The best Chief Executive Reviews were those that had little format initially on the understanding that the process would be firmed up as each six monthly review took place. At the first Chief Executive Review action plans for securing appropriate improvements were agreed, which in some cases involved developing information systems for the desired results areas before self-assessment and subsequent improvement actions could be taken. Consequently only elements of the Results criteria of the Model were used initially.

For the second review the teams needed to have some trend data and if possible some evidence of improvements. The discussion centred on actual performance and the key enablers impacting on that performance from which the second round of continuous improvement action plans emerged. As a result of undergoing the second round of reviews the teams moved towards using the RADAR logic, most of the results criteria and some of the enabler criteria of the Model. With each subsequent review more of the Model was used until the whole Model sub-criteria, RADAR logic and the scoring matrix were applied, a development that took at least two years to realise.

For some teams starting simple involved using the Model to tackle a particular complex issue. One such example was applying the relevant aspects of the Model to a benefits realisation exercise. For the department involved, the original business case contained objectives that were too loose to support the measurement of progress and so the team adopted the aforementioned approach by determining the customer, people, society and key performance results areas for the following objectives;

- To maximise the quality and effectiveness of clinical care
- To maximise efficiency and service delivery and
- To maximise the integration of service delivery with academic research and development

Once the desired results areas were determined the benefits realisation team were able to commence a first self-assessment to demonstrate performance prior to the planned change in services (which involved relocating to a new building and integrating previously discrete services) and on a six monthly basis thereafter. Applying the Model to this discrete project enabled people to understand the concepts and structure more readily than it had done formerly when the teams tried to use the whole of the Model at once. In addition, the message that the Model should be used by the team *to manage,* rather than them *feeling managed* by the Model was best attained when its concepts and structure were implemented in an incremental, specific and useful way.

Lastly starting simple was a challenge in some areas because healthcare personnel were so enthused by the concept that they embarked upon too many improvement projects in the first instance. Consequently, efforts were diluted and people felt 'burned-out'. Avoiding this hurdle was supported by using expert facilitation, as it ensured that where necessary objective prioritisation of self-assessment and improvement efforts occurred.

## Prioritising efforts

Given that many users of the Model are often overwhelmed by the amount of results areas and areas for improvements identified during the first round of self-assessment, a prioritisation tool has been developed by Centre for Excellence Development (CEO) at Salford University to deal with this particular difficulty. In essence, the tool advises healthcare personnel to use six criteria for prioritising efforts towards continuous improvement. The six criteria are the

- *Must do's*
- *High volume*
- *High cost*
- *High profile*
- *High risk*
- *High intuition.*

The *Must dos* relate to the government directives and legislative criteria that a healthcare organisation must fulfil as a basic requirement. *High volume* results areas are those that affect the most patients, and *High cost* the ones that may affect most patients or alternatively affect only a small number of patients but consume so much of the organisation's resources that they are worthy of prioritisation. *High profile* would relate to areas that are known to be sensitive amongst society, examples would include issues that have emerged from national concerns relating to healthcare practices. *High risk* clearly relates to the level of risk assigned to a result area should improvement actions not occur, and *High intuition* includes those aspects of healthcare that the users of the Model have a 'gut' feel that they should be prioritised for early improvement actions. It may be that high intuition is associated with gaining the support of a key individual or a whole team should the area be a long-standing issue within the department or organisation.

Using the prioritisation tool means that the chosen results areas would need to be scored in relation to the number of criteria they impact on. Furthermore, applying the matrix benefits from some element of weighting that the team using the tool assigns to each criterion. It may be that the 'must dos' would carry a weight of five and the remainder a range from four to two. The total scores for each result area would then be calculated and the areas prioritised for improvement actions be the ones with the highest scores. Table 6.1 provides an example of the concept for illustrative purposes.

| Criteria ➡️   Results area | Must dos (*5) | High volume (*3) | High cost (*2) | High profile (*4) | High risk (*4) | High intuition (*2) | Total score |
|---|---|---|---|---|---|---|---|
| Waiting lists | 5 | 3 | 2 | 4 | 4 | 2 | **20** |
| Complaints | 5 | | 2 | 4 | | 2 | **13** |
| Vacancy rates | | | 2 | 4 | 4 | 2 | **12** |

\* Weighting score (for illustration purposes only)

**Table 6.1  An illustration for applying CED, Salford University prioritisation matrix**

Using the prioritisation matrix would cause some anxiety amongst healthcare personnel as in the main they aspire to '*being all things to all people*', but this is tiring and not conducive to incremental continuous improvement. It is far better to do some things well and then progress to improving other areas, than to try and improve everything all at once resulting in little or no overall improvement.   Progressing towards using the EFQM Excellence Model on a day to day basis involves moving away from 'fire-fighting' to managing thereby implying that chosen results areas will be managed [better] and other areas probably subject to dealing with the urgent rather than the important, as is often the case.

Inherent within the concept of incremental continuous improvement is the setting of appropriate targets, which is another area that healthcare personnel often require assistance or guidance in.

### Setting sensible targets

Once the areas for immediate improvement actions have been identified it is important to set appropriate targets that motivate people and are associated with more successful outcomes.   Experience to date has recognised that healthcare personnel often strive to be the best, despite their constraints in terms of time and other resources. Whilst the aspiration is commendable it can be very damaging in relation to the journey towards excellence.

An example, which illustrates inappropriate target setting, comes from a delegate attending an Excellence development workshop held in January 2001. As part of a groupwork session, the delegates were asked to determine whether activities and/or initiatives they were involved in had all the elements of the RADAR logic.  During the feedback one delegate explained the details regarding a project to eliminate cancelled operations within the Ear, Nose and Throat department.   At the time the workshop was held there were approximately twenty-four cancelled operations each week. The reasons for the cancelled operations included medical and non-medical elements.

When asked what improvement target should be set, the delegate replied '*a target of no cancelled operations in any given week*'. Hence, the team would be expected to strive for total elimination of cancelled operations in the first instance. Whilst the goal is admirable, the effects of setting a goal at the level of perfection can be very demotivating and damaging. For instance, say the team worked extremely hard to reduce cancelled operations and managed to achieve a level of seventeen cancellations in a normal week, would the team celebrate success or failure? The answer from the workshop was that the achievement of seventeen per week would be associated with failure when the target was no cancellations in a given week. This would have been irrespective of the efforts deployed to reach seventeen a week, not a message conducive for motivating people towards further improvement and for rewarding their previous efforts in this area.

In contrast, if the team set a goal of nineteen cancellations in an average week and then still managed to achieve seventeen, the delegates were asked 'What would the effect be then?' The reply was that achieving seventeen in relation to a target of nineteen would more likely be associated with a feeling of success and a motivation towards further improvement than the target of none. In line with this thinking, the next target may be to achieve fifteen cancellations a week, presuming that it is easier to make a bigger impact initially than it would be to do so at later stages of the journey. To sum up then, the advice is to set incremental, stretch targets that will motivate the team towards improvement actions whilst creating opportunities for celebrating success. Obviously this approach is not suitable for some of the 'must dos' which tend to be associated with given targets irrespective of whether they relate to incremental improvements or not.

Another example, which demonstrates incremental target setting but describes a slightly different approach, comes from a surgical directorate whose outpatients department was falling behind on its national targets. To explain there were seven outpatients departments in the directorate of which none were achieving the national target of a <13week wait for an outpatient appointment. However, one department was almost achieving it, 4 departments were achieving it in 60-79% of cases and two departments in 40-59% of cases. The target set by the manager was that all the departments would reach the national target by the end of the following year. Again, whilst the aspiration was commendable the reality of achieving it was questionable. Therefore it would be highly likely that the people within the surgical directorate would be dealing with feelings of failure rather than success despite the intensity of their efforts.

The advice therefore, with regards to achieving incremental continuous improvement, (in this case) would be for the manager to set a target for the one department nearest the national target to achieve it first. Within the same year it may be appropriate to strive for two of the four departments achieving <13week outpatient appointment times in 60-79% of cases to also reach the national target. Thereby implying that target setting for improving the remaining two departments in the 60-79% bracket and the two areas in the 40-59% bracket would be relative to securing anticipated improvements rather than achieving national targets. The approach feels uncomfortable, especially where given national targets exist. However, it is better to make tangible differences in fewer areas than it is to try and change the world in one round of improvement activities an aspiration, which often results in diluted efforts and little or no change in performance regarding the achievement of national targets. Once the initial areas have achieved the national targets efforts could then be deployed to apply the learning to the remaining departments requiring improvement action so that they reach the level of performance relative to the national targets.

Consequently, improvement efforts, in relation to meeting targets needs to be ongoing thereby suggesting that once an organisation embarks upon using the EFQM Excellence Model to improve healthcare, it has no option but to stick to it for the benefit of its customers, people, society and all other stakeholders.

### Sticking at it

'*Sticking at it*' is the most vital element of the journey towards excellence. Especially as healthcare personnel often feel disillusioned with the repeated previous short-term initiatives purported as being the answer to everything. Despite the despondency people working within healthcare do want to find and use a management tool that will make excellence happen. The EFQM Excellence Model is such a tool but it requires the commitment of everyone to make it a success. Remember it is the people who make excellence happen, not the EFQM Excellence Model. However, achieving excellence requires healthcare leaders to be visible and apply relentless efforts in the pursuit of the ultimate goal.

It could be argued that healthcare is unique because everyone who works within it wants to see improvements in the service, a valuable and enviable asset that is worthy of being nurtured and utilised to the full. Nevertheless, the goal is a challenging one that needs everyone to '*stick at it*' if it is to be attained. There is no place for people who put unnecessary hurdles in front of those striving to make a difference. Instead efforts should be deployed to support the people who genuinely work towards making it happen. Activities that can help include regular quality award ceremonies that celebrate success and create an environment that enables the sharing of learning and avoids *'reinventing the wheel'*. Suggestion schemes that encourage people to put forward and develop their ideas for improvements and regular words of encouragement for people sustaining the drive for excellence, irrespective of their seniority within the organisation. Leaders, managers and front-line employees all need praise, support and encouragement to spur them towards excellence.

However, striving for excellence is not for the faint-hearted and no illusions have been made throughout this book regarding the challenge of striving for excellence in healthcare and the worthiness of the goal. Everyone within healthcare owes it to themselves, their customers and all relevant stakeholders to work towards the ultimate aim of attaining healthcare excellence. Furthermore, using the EFQM Excellence Model can support that journey providing everyone applies his or her energies to making it happen.

# References - Used

Agnew,T. (2000) "Winning hearts and minds". <u>Health Service Journal</u> 24th February 2000. P.16-17

Ainsworth,S. (2000) "Grabbed by the privates". <u>Health Service Journal</u> 13th July 2000 P.23

Ardabell,T.R., Turjanica,M.A., Mastorovich,M.J., Hirschman,V. (1995) "Business Process Quality Management: A Step Beyond Continuous Quality Improvement". <u>MEDSURG Nursing</u> August 1995 Vo.4 No.4 P.279-288

Azzolini,M., Shillaber,J. (1993) "Internal Service Quality: Winning from the Inside Out". <u>Quality Progress</u> November 1993 P.75-78

Baker,B. (2000) "Turn the tables on blame to create opportunity". Letter. <u>Health Service Journal</u> 17th December 1998 P.21

Brannan,K. (1998) "Total quality in health care". <u>Hospital Material Management Quarterly</u> May 1998 Vol.19 No.4 P.1-8

Collard,R., Sivyer,G. (1990) "Total Quality". <u>Personnel Management</u> Factsheet 29. May 1990

Crosby,P. (1980) "Quality is Free. The art of making quality certain". Mentor Books Penguin. New York

Dale,B.G., Boaden,R.J., Lascelles,D.M. (1994) "Total Quality Management: an overview". In Managing Quality edited by Barrie G Dale. Second edition. Prentice Hall London

Deming,W.E. (1982) "Quality, Productivity and Competitive Position". Massachusetts Institute of Technology. MA

Department of Health (1998) "A First Class Service. Quality in the new NHS". Department of Health July 1998

Department of Health (2000) "The NHS Plan. A plan for investment A plan for reform" The Stationary Office

Donabedian,A. (1980) "Explorations in Quality Assessment and Monitoring. Vol.1 The Definition of Quality and Approaches to its Assessment". Health Administration Press, Ann Arbor, Michigan

Eaton,L. (2000) "Getting back on its feet"' <u>Health Service Journal</u> 1st June 2000. P.7

EFQM (1997) "Self-Assessment. Guidelines for Companies". The European Foundation for Quality Management Brussels

EFQM (European Foundation for Quality Management) Web-site (1999) Site accessed 13th March 1999 www.efqm.org

EFQM (European Foundation for Quality Management) Web-site (1999) Site accessed 10th June 1999 www.efqm.org

EFQM (1999a) "The EFQM Excellence Model. Public and Voluntary Sectors Version". The European Foundation for Quality Management, Brussels

EFQM (1999b) "Assessing Excellence. A Practical Guide for Self-Assessment.". The European Foundation for Quality Management, Brussels

EFQM (2000) "The European Quality Award". Handbook downloaded from the web-site www.efqm.org 28th December 2000

Evenden,R., Anderson,G. (1992) "Making the Most of People". Addison-Wesley Wokingham, England.

Gordon,J.R. (1987) "A Diagnostic Approach To Organisational Behaviour". Second Edition. Allyn and Bacon,Inc. London

Handy,C. (1985) "Understanding Organisations." Penguin Business Books. Middlesex

Hunter, D. (1997) "Wrongly held to account". Health Service Journal 8th May 1997 P.17

Jackson,S., Freer,J., France,B. (1998) "Managing change and learning that quality is a journey not a destination". British Journal of Health Care Management Vol.4 No.11 November P.528 - 533

Jackson,S. (1999) "Exploring the possible reasons why the UK Government commended the EFQM excellence model as the framework for delivering governance in the new NHS'. International Journal of Health Care Quality Assurance Vol.12 No.6 P.244-243

Jackson, S. (2000) "Clinical governance using a business excellence model." British Journal of Midwifery October 2000, Vol.8 No.10 P.645-65

Juran, J.M. (ed) (1988) "Quality Control Handbook". McGraw-Hill, New York

McIntosh, K. (1998) "£100m a year 'wasted' on prescriptions for drug treatments 'of doubtful value'". Health Service Journal 29th October 1998 P.3

McIntosh, K. (1999) "Wham BAMM". Health Service Journal 10th June 1999 P.12

McIntosh,K., Shifrin,T., Thompson,M., Davies,P. (2000) "NHS 'short of local leaders'." Health Service Journal 6th July 2000. P.14

May,A. (1998) "Take it up with the kipper". Health Service Journal 1st October 1998 P.22-21

Maynard, A., Sheldon, T. (1997) "Time to turn the tide". Health Service Journal 25th September 1997 P.25

Maynard,A. (2000) "Bleating up the wrong tree". Health Service Journal 7th December 2000. P.18-19

Megginson,L.C., Mosley,D.C., Pietri.Jnr.P.H. (1989) "Management Concepts and Applications". Third Edition. Harper & Row. London

Myers, P. (1999) "Making their marker". Health Service Journal 21st January 1999 P.28

NHS Executive (1999a) "Governance in the new NHS". Health Service Circular 1999/123 21st May 1999

NHS Executive (1999b) "Clinical Governance: in the new NHS". Health Service Circular 1999/065 16th March 1999

Oakland,J.S. (1989) "Total Quality Management". Heinemann Professional Publishing Oxford

Ovretveit,J. (1998) 'Proving and improving the quality of the national health services'. The New Face of the NHS, Ed. P Spurgeon; 2nd edition, London: Royal Society of Medicine Press.

Øvretveit,J. (1999) "Integrated Quality Development in Public Healthcare. *A Comparison of Six Hospitals Quality Programmes and a Practical Theory for Quality Development.* Norwegian Medical Association's Publication Series: Continuing Education and Quality Improvement P.O. Box 1151 Sentrum, 0107 Oslo, Norway

Peratec. (1994) "Total Quality Management. The key to business improvement". Second Edition. A Peratec executive briefing. Chapman & Hall ISBN 0 412 58640-1

Porter,L., Tanner,S.J. (1996) "Assessing Business Excellence. A guide to self-assessment." Butterworth Heineman Linacre House, Jordan Hill, Oxford OX2 8DP

Smith, S. (1986) "How to take Part in the Total Quality Revolution: A Management Guide". London: PA Management Consultants

Stahr,H., Bulman,B., Stead,M. (2000) "The Excellence Model in the Health Sector. Sharing Good Practice". KINGSHAM Press, Chichester, West Sussex

Wakeley,M. (1997) "Quality commitment". Health Service Journal 7th August 1997 P.29

White, M. (1999) "Tory campaign to free the Manifesto Promise One". Health Service Journal 28th October 1999 P.21

Wright,A. (1997) "Public service quality: Lessons not learned". Total Quality Management October 1997 Vol.8 No.5 P.313-320

# Index